Help
for the
Helpers

RUTH M. GEIMAN, PH. D.

Help
for the
Helpers

HOW TO HELP YOUR CHILDREN WITH LEARNING PROBLEMS
TO BE HIGHLY SUCCESSFUL IN SCHOOL AND LIFE

TATE PUBLISHING
AND ENTERPRISES, LLC

Published by Tate Publishing & Enterprises, LLC
127 E. Trade Center Terrace | Mustang, Oklahoma 73064 USA
1.888.361.9473 | www.tatepublishing.com

Tate Publishing is committed to excellence in the publishing industry. The company reflects the philosophy established by the founders, based on Psalm 68:11,
"The Lord gave the word and great was the company of those who published it."

Book design copyright © 2016 by Tate Publishing, LLC. All rights reserved.
Cover design by Albert Ceasar Compay
Interior design by Shieldon Alcasid

Published in the United States of America
ISBN: 978-1-68187-283-4
Education / Special Education / Learning Disabilities
15.12.07

Table of Contents

Table of Contents

Table of Contents

Table of Contents

Foreword

A Special Note to Parents from the Author

My wish for you as you read this book is that it will help guide you on your journey of helping your own children learn in spite of possible physical disabilities that may have masked their true ability. As parents of children with learning disabilities and processing problems, your lives have probably been an adventure. Adventures include a lot of trials and unmapped journeys. My hope is that this book can encourage all of you on your journey by giving you a guide of what to expect as you go forward.

Life can contain moments of sorrow and times of peace. Sometimes there are special high points of bliss and happiness. Belief systems help us through the hard times so that we have the opportunity to experience the special times of life. Celebrating the good times and remembering them through the difficult times can help us in life. However, my strength has been in knowing that this world is temporary. The troubles here are difficult and real and must be handled, but I believe that a very loving and caring Father guides not only my steps, but can guide *yours,* too.

This book will not bring instant happiness, peace, prosperity, or calm. In fact, you may become upset, discouraged, angry, and unhappy for a while. Much of what I am going to tell you, you probably have already guessed or figured out by yourself. Years of research and helping people have led me to write down what can empower you to go forward on your journey, confident in your ability. You will know that your special person's inner desire to communicate and be successful was thwarted by an unseen and sometimes unknown enemy. Hopefully, that enemy will be conquered as you help your children overcome the weird issues that have puzzled them and those who have tried to help them.

I will serve as a guide who has gone along the path before you and can help point out known problems and difficulties. Unfortunately, guides cannot see into the future and predict unknown dangers. As a guide, I will encourage you to travel through some very hard places. In order to change, you and your children will have to work and work hard. Crying is expected. Anger is normal. Discouragement will present itself. No amount of words or preparation can remove the sorrow that you and your children have experienced. Prayer and support from others can help you both as you pass through these deep times.

Are you and your children ready for a change? Sometimes you will be happy you helped your children change. Other times you will wish you had never even picked up this book. Prepare to set the book aside and take breaks (even long breaks) as you need them. Helping your children is not an easy task. This task will demand a lot of work. In fact, this book is an introduction to a possible set of books. In the next books, I plan to go into much more detail about how you can overcome or avoid the problems your children face.

I will be using stories throughout this book. I have found two things to help me personally through the storms: my belief that God cares and my equally strong belief that laughter and crying and even anger help us get through them. Use your faith and emotions to help you and your children.

I do not know you, but I do know that God does, no matter who you are. You do not need to be a Christian to use this book. God will help you when this book does not. He can support you and your children when your family and friends cannot. He knows what good He has planned for you and your children when you may not see any good. You can learn about God who loves every single person on earth whether you know Him or not. Christian churches, radio stations, and television networks have speakers about Him. The Bible reveals Him. He wants to have you know Him and trust Him. Best wishes in discovering Him.

Here is a story from my life: I frequently am asked to tell faculty about my research. I include stories from my life in those presentations. I was presenting to faculty from a Catholic school. I told of my frustration and how I had called out to God to send me someone to help me with my son and daughter. A man laughed and said, "And God sent you YOU."

I believe God will do this for you, too. When you have no answers, He will definitely show *you* what to do. Your answers will help you immediately. You will be amazed how many people will be encouraged and helped by your faithfulness and care of your specific children. You are specially gifted to care for them.

You have been given these particular children because God knew you were exactly the best people to care for them. Trust that God will also give you the skill, patience, and wisdom to help them correctly. Listen to what others write and say, but follow what you know is best for your children. You are your children's experts. They are different from every other person on earth.

There are similarities, but there will be important differences that will mean adjustment of ideas to fit them. God bless you in your special service!

Special thanks to my children Eric, Drew, Christina, and Calvin who lived through these discoveries and recoveries. They were present to encourage many students who have successfully learned how to help themselves learn. Thanks to the many parents and students who shared their times of discovery and recovery with us and helped me to help others along this path.

Many thanks to my wonderful family editors: Michelle, Drew, Christian, Bradley, and Eric Geiman, Dori Winkel, Marcy Drescher, Dannette Richards and Jerry and Bill Nolte. Their comments - kind, yet thorough - helped me fashion a readable book for you. Thanks to all the readers who read and commented back on the drafts of the book. Your input was a major part of this writing process.

Chapter 1

The Geiman Method

Why the Geiman Method was invented

When two of my children were diagnosed with learning problems, I went to the parent conference[1] and was greeted by their principal. Before the meeting, we talked. Here is what I remember of that conversation:

Me: Just tell me what to do for my children, and I will do it.

Principal: Yes, just tell us what to do, and we'll do it.

Me: You mean --- we don't have a clue what to do!

Principal: No one does.

That began a journey that continues still today. I was terrified. I did not know how to help my children. At one point, I literally screamed at God to send someone to help me help my children. As I told this story to a group of

---

[1] Different states and school districts have different names for this formal conference each school year. The meeting refers to the educational planning meeting between school professionals and parents.

educators, a man laughed and blurted out, "And God sent you – you!"

In the past we did not know about all of these issues. A retired teacher read the book and said, "I had a fourth grader who had these problems. We did not know what to do. We just passed him along. I could have helped him with this information."

Teachers and administrators could not know about these problems because I found them in the *neurological* literature. These are documented physical problems that seriously impair learning. Now that we know about the processing issues we can correct for them in educational settings. Then we can help your children learn to their full potential.

I have been asked why each child needs to be tested. An analogy with glasses will demonstrate why: When we get an eye examination, we may need glasses. We need the correct glasses for our specific eyes, not for someone else's. The prescription must fit us. In the same way, millions of disruptions could occur in processing, but your children only need the compensations (corrections) for their specific problems, not for all of the known issues. Their prescription must fit them precisely.

Another concern is how long the compensations will be needed. Just as glasses are needed to continuously correct for eye issues, so these compensations will be needed for the processing issues. The issues may change slightly as your children grow, but their need for the compensations will not go away.

For years, I have worked, helping others. Recently, we found out that my grandson has these issues, and now I am determined to revisit the problems and learn how to correct for the problems even better than before.[2]

Problems treated by the Geiman Method

This book is dedicated to all people who struggle with the problems of garbling of information. Garbling of information can be called dyslexia, auditory processing problems, learning disabilities, attention deficit disorder, and many other names that are classifications for learning and social issues. The research about these learning difficulties does not have accurate descriptions of the problems themselves nor does it include details that are essential for correcting the problems.

The solutions are missing. The answers are simply to take longer and to simplify the material. These two answers aggravate the problems rather than correct for them. I knew

---

[2]He improved in one school year from being placed into 2nd grade to qualifying for gifted and talented instruction.

that my two children – later three children - were bright and capable. Somehow they had to learn how to get around seeing unpredictably, hearing irregularly, writing imperfectly, speaking inexactly, and retrieving the wrong information from their long- and short-term memory. We struggled for years to determine how to show their intelligence and ability. The search for additional help continues, but the problems of processing are vast. I believe that God sent you – you for your specific children. I will tell you what I discovered. In addition, I will add what others have taught me.

Development of the Geiman Method

The Geiman Method grew as I helped hundreds of people. They heard about my children's success in learning. Professionals and families sought me out to help people with serious issues. Many people advanced the program by helping me discover how they learned and demonstrated their ability.

While I was helping hundreds of both adults and children learn how to overcome problems associated with learning, people consistently asked me to write about what we were doing. The first two people that I helped were my own two children. Today, both are highly successful adults. Next I helped hundreds of adults and children through the Bureau for Vocational Rehabilitation (BVR) and through helping clients of an attorney for Americans for Basic Legal Equality (ABLE). In addition, I helped patients of vision specialists. I published the information, received awards (among them a letter of commendation from Barbara Bush), and presented this information at many peer reviewed conferences. I taught the method at Wright State University, Dayton, Ohio. Then I lost much of my own vision. Now I am experiencing first-hand the hard knocks school of visual distortion!

Finally, I am helping my grandson. He has inspired me to write this down so that no one else has to go on this journey alone. I am writing this book for you - the parents, grandparents, aunts, uncles, or other interested people who are working side by side with people who have processing or learning problems.

If you are a teacher, administrator, or a person with disabilities, feel free to apply the concepts given in this book as they fit your needs. I hope that school districts will give this book to parents so that parents know how to help their children overcome processing issues and successfully and effectively demonstrate their ability in school settings. If you received this book and your children do not have a diagnosis, you can request an evaluation of your own children in writing at their school district to begin the process of getting help for your children.

I have helped hundreds of people successfully overcome processing problems. The problems are also called dyslexia, learning disabilities, ADHD, and many other names. By treating the processing problems as physical problems and by assuming excellent intelligence from the people who have them, I have been able to help adults and children overcome processing issues.

I am the mother and teacher of people with these problems. In addition, I have worked with professionals and people with problems as well as researching the relevant literature concerning processing difficulties. These three roles of mother, teacher, and researcher give me a unique view of processing problems and corrections of them. The Geiman Method and the compensations listed in the *General Processing Inventory (GPI)* were developed based on these experiences.

The *GPI* is the special standardized test I wrote to document the serious errors that are preventing people from learning. As a mother, I know that the compensations listed in the *GPI* are essential and nonnegotiable. As a researcher, I know that the *GPI* compensations are valid and overcome the problems that they are designed to overcome. As a teacher, I know that the *GPI* compensations are compatible with good educational practices and classroom procedures.

The processing problems must be directly addressed. Solving your children's specific problems will be strenuous work. It will require your determination, but also your children's strength and ingenuity. Stubbornness is a great quality for people who have these problems! The journey is long and sometimes extremely difficult. Take heart. You are not alone.

Possibly, your children have just been diagnosed with a learning disability and/or you have been invited to a parent/teacher meeting to help develop the educational plan for the next school year. You may have concerns about your children's success both in the coming year and in their future lives. One concern is whether the diagnosis is accurate. You know that your children struggle at times, but is learning disabilities the correct label for what they are experiencing?

A label is required to gain special assistance at school. You will continue to have input into your children's educational adaptations all through grade school to high school. Use the information from this book and the results of the *GPI* to be sure your children receive the best possible education to match their needs.

In this chapter, I introduce you to the Geiman Method which has demonstrated success in helping people overcome learning disabilities. Here I will answer your questions by discussing the following topics:

- Your children's disability is real (the name does not matter)
- Your children's problems are probably physical
- Your children may be extremely impaired (comparison to Helen Keller)
- Processing problems are altered perceptions (an example)
- What you can expect
- What the Geiman Method is
- Why rapid success is possible
- How the Geiman Method can be enacted
- What should already be completed

Your children's disability is real (the name does not matter)

Your children may have received the diagnosis of dyslexia, learning disabilities, auditory problems, writing issues, memory lapses, or speech irregularities. The name is not important, but the name allows your children access to special educational opportunities. You may be concerned that a label may trap your children in a special educational system that will not allow them full access to educational opportunities now and in the future. This book is designed to help you, as a parent, successfully assist your children's teachers in giving your children the best possible educational experience as well as helping your children overcome their problems so that they can benefit from the education they receive. This will prevent them from being trapped into a substandard education by well-meaning professionals with partial information.

Your children's entrance into special education via their diagnoses gives you an opportunity to participate in planning your children's education. You are an equal partner with their educational professionals in collaborating to determine what opportunities your children need. You are the experts on your children; school personnel are experts on the opportunities available to your children. Together you can develop the best plan of education possible for your children. The label is the doorway into matching educational resources with your children's needs.

Your children's problems are probably physical

That there is a problem with how your children learn can be clearly documented through the results of the *GPI* and the rest of the tests that your children's school personnel used. The approaches to take concerning those problems will determine their success. Until recently, learning problems were considered to be cognitive or mental problems, which meant that learning itself would be difficult. My research and experiences with hundreds of people demonstrate that many of their learning problems are physical problems. These physical problems will not disappear. Therefore the goal of special educational methods must be to get through or around the physical problems and give your children tools and compensations to use that allow them to show their true cognitive ability.

Your children may be extremely impaired (comparison to Helen Keller)

Helen Keller was born with normal abilities, but became blind and deaf when she was very young. With the help of Anne Sullivan, a dedicated teacher who learned how to translate information to Helen, she was able to graduate from college and lead a successful and fulfilled life. The methods Anne used were innovative for their times. Deciding Helen could learn was the first step toward success.

When we compare what your children are dealing with to what Helen Keller's problems were, we see striking similarities and differences. Like Helen, your children cannot process material heard or seen. In fact, they probably cannot *see* or *write* accurately. In addition, they also may not *hear* and *speak* accurately. Also, they may not retrieve material from their *memory systems* accurately. They are impaired in as many as six physical areas, not just two like Helen Keller. The accommodations they usually receive in special educational systems are limited to additional time and tutoring. Neither accommodation addresses or compensates for the massive processing garbling that is the root cause of their educational disturbance.

Just as Helen Keller and her helper Anne Sullivan spent a great deal of time and effort to learn how Helen needed to learn, you and your children will have to spend a great deal of time and effort to learn how they learn. Then learning how to use their specific adaptations will take even more time and effort. Getting around the physical problems is similar to learning how to read when blind or learning how to write when paralyzed. You will be helping your children learn how to hear accurately while learning to communicate. Your children will have to consistently check their speech to be sure it is accurate, too. Memory retrieval methods must be learned and used. Memory storage must be adjusted to accommodate for irregularities that must be avoided. Knowing which areas are malfunctioning is accomplished by using the *GPI*. Then the appropriate adjustments to your children's education can be made. These adjustments are called compensations and recommendations in the *GPI* results.

Treating the physical root causes of the learning disturbances and teaching your children to compensate for the garbling that occurs are the fundamental tools used in the Geiman Method. Your children will be able to demonstrate their ability and be successful in their education, their social interactions, and their later adult life. Without adaptation training, they will continue to make serious communication errors that will prevent accurate interactions with others and will create problems with both learning and understanding. They need adjustments and compensations so that they can overcome their processing problems just as Helen Keller overcame hers.

Processing problems are altered perceptions (an example)

For years, people with your children's problems have been left to struggle through an educational process that did not know how to help them learn. By slightly adjusting this educational process, your children will be able to learn. Your children may be just as impaired as blind or deaf children. Their problems can be equally physical. For example, your children's vision may be altering the letters on a page. This means that instead of seeing the three letters of *CAT*, as most people see them, your children may see them as *TAC, ACT, TCA, ATC*, or *CTA*. Then the *c* may look like an *e*, so they have six additional ways the word could look. The letters may reverse. Some of the letters may reverse and others stay the same. The *T* may look like an *F*. The *A* may look like a *V* or a *W*. After considering all the different possibilities for distortion of a single three-letter word, we know that your children may see the same word in over 1000 different ways. No wonder reading is so difficult! Your children need to know what is malfunctioning and how to get around the errors.

What you can expect

The good news is that the Geiman Method can help your children move from failure to success in their educational and social world. They can learn to be able to function in a world that does not adjust to them by learning how to adjust to that world. The problems are not going to go away. Your children will learn to cope with them and to adjust their processing so that communication is more accurate.

Your children have been working around these problems without accurate assistance. Your children are performing in a system that is confusing and irregular. The irregular input and output of material make learning extremely difficult. Your children cannot demonstrate the excellent intellectual ability it takes to function in a world that has all this garbling. When the compensations are applied, your children's true ability will be seen. Expect to see an immense improvement.

What the Geiman Method is

The four keys to success through the Geiman Method are

- Identification of the specific processing errors that affect your children using the *GPI* examination
- Development of an individualized compensation program based on those documented errors
- Rapid review in all subject areas and application of the *GPI* compensations
- Reintroduction into regular educational settings

During the next few weeks, your children should be tested with the *GPI*[3] (unless they have already been tested with the *GPI*) to uncover their specific errors. The *GPI* will help sort through thousands of different ways that people can misprocess information. In the *GPI*, the specific errors are organized into these six categories:

- Vision
- Hearing
- Writing
- Speech
- Retrieval from long-term memory storage
- Retrieval from short-term memory storage

The specific errors in each of the above six categories are similar. Garbling of information includes:

- Reversing
- Substituting
- Repeating
- Dropping
- Adding symbols, letters, and words

---

[3] Available from the author. See Appendix B.

- Many additional errors

Then for six to eighteen months, your children should review all previous educational material. Your children may complete this review at school in a special educational setting. When that is not possible, you can complete the review at home. Ideally, they should complete the review and then catch up with their class as their last stage of the review. However, sometimes, they will be required to do their regular classroom work during the review.

As your children review, they will learn to overcome their specific errors by starting at material that is very simple. They will review rapidly and meticulously. As they review, they will practice the compensations from the *GPI* test results to learn how to compensate for their errors.

They will try different ways to remember and to memorize. For example, they can learn math adding, subtracting, multiplying, and dividing facts by observing patterns through the Geiman Method. I developed eight basic facts booklets to help your children sort the facts, rather than directly memorizing them.[4] Children and adults with learning problems helped develop the

---

[4] Available from the author. See Appendix B.

books by telling what they saw about the number facts, such as 4+6 or 4 × 6.

During their review, your children will review the details of reading, the grammar and punctuation for writing, and the concepts of math, science, social studies, and health. They will review spelling rules, participate in music classes, exercise in physical education programs, and express themselves through art. They will use regular textbooks and educational materials. They will review and study material from kindergarten through their grade level and one level beyond so that you and they know that they have all the tools for success.

Why rapid success is possible

Quick success is possible because your children are not cognitively impaired; they literally see, hear, speak, write, and retrieve material differently from what is meant and presented. For example, they could hear an instructor say that **Thomas Jefferson** invented the light bulb - when in fact the instructor correctly stated that **Thomas Edison** invented it. When they answer a multiple choice exam question, they may write the answer **b** for **d**. When they read the number **17**, they sometimes see a reversal **71** and say, **27**. No wonder their educational progress is impaired!

Once your children understand how impaired their processing is, they can learn to adjust. They practice adjusting as they pass through the review material. They will go back to the beginning of the educational process and use the books for math, science, reading, health, English, spelling, and social studies. They will review all the topics and apply the compensations based on the *GPI* results. They will be amazed that they can learn to adjust for the garbling. They can learn to identify when they are processing inaccurately. They can learn how to check for their personal error patterns, find them, and correct for them.

The key to success is that their specific processing errors are identified accurately. Now they need to learn exactly how their vision, hearing, writing, and speaking processes are not reliable. They need to find out how to make the processes more accurate and how to adjust for the remaining inaccuracies they perceive. Just as a person who is paralyzed cannot write and needs help communicating in writing, your children have to learn to adjust, too. Just as a person with visual handicaps cannot read, your children may not see what is actually on the page and may not read accurately. Then their specific reading adjustments must be made. Also, if your children misspeak and mishear, they must learn to check input and output constantly and consistently to accurately understand conversations. In addition, your children may need to carefully monitor and adjust their memory storage and retrieval methods.

How the Geiman Method can be enacted

I have included a brief *GPI* screening[5] to determine if your children need to take the full *GPI.* Follow the directions in reading the screening to your children. If they make five or more errors, they need to learn how to adjust their environment. They should be evaluated with the entire three-hour *GPI* to find out how they need to adjust.

Next, your children need to review all the material that was presented to them to learn how to use the compensations necessary for learning.

- They will need to learn when they are reading inaccurately.
- They need to check for inaccuracy in writing.
- They can learn what they need to do when they are listening to someone speak.

---

[5] See Appendix D

- They can recognize the signs that they are not saying what they thought they were saying.
- They can develop ways to check that they are remembering and following information just given.
- They can adjust the way they memorize and store information.

As they adjust, first they may experience anger and frustration as they learn the compensations. They may be annoyed that no one noticed the root problems for their struggling. They may be tempted to quit because the process seems too long and difficult. It is important that they work with an adult to learn how to overcome and work with the way they process material.

A special education setting may work well for your children while they are learning their compensations. Working with other students who are also overcoming their processing errors is very encouraging. All students can share their successes and challenges as they learn to compensate for processing errors that prevented them from communicating accurately. Your children may need six to eighteen months to overcome the problems.[6]

What should already be completed

If you suspect that your children have learning problems, you should have requested – in writing - an evaluation from their school psychologist. This evaluation will help define the learning problems and how to adapt for them. If you have not had an evaluation, request one ***in writing.*** A verbal request does not start the process. You must write your request.

After the evaluation, you should be invited to a formal meeting to determine the educational plan for your children. You are an equal partner with the other professionals who will be attending. Before the meeting, write down what you want to request for your children and check off the requests as you voice them. Give your list and the *GPI* recommendations to the **moderator** of the meeting as you leave. Keep a copy for yourself.

In Appendix C, I have a review of the entire book. You can use the review to help you make a decision about how you want to read this book. Also look at Appendix D and administer the *GPI* screening and act on the information.

---

[6] See Appendix B for details about evaluation and training.

Chapter 2
Reading Adjustments for Visual Distortion

As parents, you can be very frustrated when you see your children struggle with reading. The focus of this chapter is on how you can reduce that frustration as you help your children learn how to read effectively and efficiently. They may have spent years attempting to read. **Why** they cannot learn to read is very important. They may not read because they have processing problems which cause visual distortions. These visual distortions are the reason for their failure to read. You can help them overcome or compensate for the visual problems and show them that reading is possible. Analysis of possible sources of reading failure is the first step toward helping your children become successful readers.

Reading is one of the fundamental ways to gain knowledge. This skill is essential for them during their education now and will continue to be a critical skill they use throughout their lives. Because visual distortion can make reading intensely difficult, adapting for the visual distortion is critical. Dyslexia is the most frequently used term for the distortion. In this chapter we discuss the following:

- Visual distortion defined
- Alternate methods of reading information
- Essential compensation skills
- Checklist for specific reading errors
- Next steps
- Information for the instructional planning meeting[7]

Visual distortion defined

Your children probably have a great understanding of the reading process; however, their visual distortions prevent them from applying that knowledge. There are many ways visual distortion can affect reading. Their visual distortions may change the appearance of letters, symbols, words, and even whole pages of material. Reading is quite confusing with all of these changes. Correcting for visual distortions is critical in learning how to read.

Some of the ways that vision can be distorted include the following: your children may not see the endings of words, letters may be scrambled, and words may change as they view them. In addition, the page may appear as if it is swirling. The page they are reading may suddenly become

---

[7] Different states and school districts have different names for this formal conference each school year. The meeting refers to the educational planning meeting between school professionals and parents.

black. All these distortions may continue even though your children may learn to get around them. Until your children are able to correct for their specific distortions, they need the best compensation for reading failure – read everything to them and with them.

Even though correcting for visual distortion is critical, your children should also review how to read to be sure that they have not missed some important steps in learning how to read. While reading with them, other reading issues may appear. These are discussed in the next chapter. They are common to all readers and should be considered, but are not part of the visual distortion.

Reading for fun isn't fun when reading isn't fun

Many children learn how to read by reading stories that are written for entertainment. These *fun* stories do not work for children who have visual distortion. Your children cannot see the words on the page. Reading for fun is not an option when reading is not fun at all. Your children will love to hear *you* read stories for fun, but until they are able to read without help, you will have to use the following alternate reading methods and compensations.

Alternate methods of reading information
Read their own words

You will definitely have to help your children by trying some very basic skill development procedures. The first method is to have them read their own words. Have your children tell you anything. Write down their words. Read them back to them. Then have the children read the words. Play this game with them as often as they will let you. Then write their words again and have them read them back. Be sure to avoid pressuring them. Help them with any words as soon as they pause. After just a few seconds if they pause while they are reading, give them the word that is confusing them - unless they ask you to wait.

When your children understand that reading is hearing what someone else said and is like talking on paper, you are ready to go to the next step. Notice that the writing process and the reading process are intricately intertwined. We will use writing with reading to assist your children. Writing is like talking and reading is like hearing what was said on paper.

The next step in this process is having them write their own words as you give them the spellings that they need. Give them the spellings without asking them to sound out the letters. Sounding out words will come later. It is too involved for beginning readers with lots of visual distortion. Writing helps your children slow down the reading process as they learn the details of the words.

Write to them

Now you can start writing a few words in notes to help them read. Write, "I love you," on a heart. Make a list of their chores and post it on the refrigerator. Have them keep track of the chores. Write more detail about each chore every week. For example: *hair, clothes, breakfast, teeth, school, homework, play, walk, bath, teeth* - could be the first list. Then on the next list write: *Comb hair, Put on clothes, Eat breakfast, Brush teeth, Go to school, Do homework, Play, Walk the dog,* etc. You are talking to your children on paper as they learn to read what you said.

Be personal and creative. Your messages are important to helping your children learn to use written words. Write notes to them. Be sure to use words that are important to them. Help them *hear* you mentally as they read your words.

Have your children write notes to people who will answer and write back to them. Let them learn to text on your phone. Help them write emails to people who will write back. Help them *talk* with writing and *listen* with reading.

Teach them Braille

Braille is another tool to help your children learn what reading is. We taught my daughter Braille to help her read. She was in fifth grade when a friend who was blind tried the method. One day, reading made sense to her. She felt the letters for the word bat, and said, "B - a - t - bat, they're words!" From then on, she could read the words on the page, too. It was still hard work, but she finally was able to understand what reading was. She did not need the Braille once she made the connection between the symbols on the page and words.

If you do not have access to teaching Braille, you can adapt this process through your writing back and forth to your children. You can tell them that writing and reading are like talking on paper- in *words*! You will notice when the reading idea becomes real. They will suddenly understand what you are trying to teach them. Be prepared to read a lot more to and with them when they suddenly realize what reading is.

Read for information that they want

Two of my children had difficulty learning how to read. My son loved sharks, so we read books we found on sharks. Soon we were reading quite technical material. At first I did most of the reading, but soon, my son wanted to read when I was busy, so he would read standing next to me and ask me, "What's this word?" When we went to aquariums, he read all the information signs. He would spend hours struggling through difficult books on sharks because he loved learning about them. Reading what my son found interesting was the key to his learning how to read independently and well.

My daughter loved cats. We were soon reading technical books about them. When a national cat show opened four blocks from our home, we went. Reading with my children for information they wanted was the way both of them began reading on their own. They did not read for fun until much later. Today, they are both college graduates who read fluently and often.

My grandson is reading about hockey at a level well above what he reads at school. He loves to learn about slap shots and stick handling. Now he has progressed to refusing to have me give him a word unless he specifically asks for it. He has been working on reading for six months now. He had me write his words and then read them. He read messages from me. He wrote his own messages. He also read the books from school (the for-fun books) and declared them all boring. When we got material he wanted, he read at adult levels.

You can find out what your children are interested in by watching and listening to them. Do they like different countries? Do they like to cook? Do they like a special animal? Do they like to hear about famous people? Keep asking them and going to the library to try out books they may like. Let them take books just to look at the pictures, too. Let them guide you into how deeply they want to read a book.

Read what they think is entertaining

Read books that your children find entertaining. Let them decide which books those are. Take them to a library (or bookstore) at least once a week. Let them take home as many books as possible. Let them try out the books to see if they like them. You can return books to the library for more if they were not entertaining to your children. Reading, whether you or they do the actual reading, is fun only when your children are enjoying it.

Let your children ask the librarian about books to read. Librarians are excellent resource people for finding books that are interesting to children. Their suggestions are invaluable in helping find material that your children will enjoy. In addition, librarians are wonderful resource people for your children's entire life.

Remember to read almost the entire selection with your children. At first, you will be doing almost all of the reading. You can have your children read a word on each page. Let them pick the word. Then you can have them read a sentence on the page. When that is getting easy, have them pick a paragraph to read. After a while, have your children read a page and then you read a page. Let them pick the page. You are the person who facilitates the reading process so that the content comes alive.

As your children read, if they pause, give them the next word unless they ask you to wait. When you are reading, follow what you are reading with your finger. Do not make them watch you, but show them where you are reading so that they can watch as their eyes will let them. Make sure the content is the focus of your reading and that reading does not interrupt the flow of the content.

Sometimes your children will need to close their eyes while you are reading. This can help the distortion slow and stop. Also, you can try covering the pages with different colored plastic sheets from plastic folders to see if the coloring helps stop and slow the distortion. Because plastic sheets can be easily scratched, change them often so that they are free from scratches. The scratches can interfere with seeing the print on the page. Reduce distortion by reducing glare and letting your children rest their eyes.

Read plays

Some children love to read plays. At first, your children will want the part with the fewest words. You will notice their confidence build as they start asking for the parts with more lines. Again, help them as soon as they pause for a word. Keep the words moving along. You might even find a play or two that your family can learn and perform for friends.

Essential compensation skills
Review learning how to read

The first compensation starts with taking the very easy reading books and showing your children how their identified errors are making reading so difficult. When you read with them out loud, track what you are reading with your finger or a pointer. Your children may not be able to watch the tracking at first or at times when the distortion is strong. Have them close their eyes to rest them and see if the distortion is reduced. Your goal is to review while teaching your children how to get around their identified visual distortion errors. I find tracking above the words works better than tracking below the words. I do not know why.

Be sure to go through a reading series that introduces how to use phonics to read. Review all the lessons about learning how to read until you are at their grade level. Then go one grade level above that. Your children's confidence is secured as they see their progress and learn to compensate for their visual distortions.

Read all the stories of the reading books. Read them quickly. You will be doing much of the reading at first. Review learning how to read so that your children can see that the reason they did not learn how to read was the visual distortion.

If your children are going through this reading review in school, assist the teachers by asking what you should read with your children at home. Read with them often. Use material that is important to them and you. I used storybooks and children's stories to read every night. Later, I read chapter books, like C.S. Lewis' children's series and my children's favorite books. Our reading was a special quiet time just before my children went to sleep. Help your children by reading with them every day.

Read most of it

At first, you will be reading most of the words. Until your children are able to self-correct, read everything with them. Soon, they will be able to recognize when they need to go back over something they read. Until they learn self-confidence, read almost everything they need to read with them. They will become independent when they have learned the compensations they need. Until then, you are helping them learn that reading is a great way to communicate and learn. You are your children's best helper in letting them learn to read. Read, read, and read to and with them!

Read together all of their homework assignments in other subjects

Science, social studies, health, math and every other subject area will be hard to read at first. You will have to read every word with your children for a while. Teach them to read the headings, the captions under the pictures, and to look at charts and maps. Chapters 5, 6, and 7 have more ideas about how to help them in content area reading. Read their subject material so that they are accurately receiving and learning the material.

Checklist for specific reading errors

You will notice that your children will make the same errors over and over. Keep track of them. Many of them were probably identified with the *GPI*. Throughout their lives, your children will continue to get to know themselves and their errors better and better. They need to learn their errors so that they can watch for them and correct for them. These are not cognitive errors. They are due to the visual distortion that occurs. Record the errors, so they become a checklist for learning to overcome the errors.

Next steps

Reading is an essential skill for school. You will soon find that your reading assistance has paid off. Your children will gradually move to the stage of just asking you to read words that are confusing. Always give the word by pointing at it and gliding your finger across it so their eyes can track what you are reading. Give the words quickly and without comment. Distortion cannot be taught away. Just give them the words!

Information for the instructional planning meeting[8]

When you are invited to the yearly meeting to plan services for your children, be sure to include reading all standardized tests to them. When they are under any pressure, the distortion will return or intensify. Also, include that all assignments below a B- are re-evaluated with someone reading the questions or problems that have errors. Teachers should also include questions that are correct by using a clean test page so that your children do not just change answers, but are truly showing their skill.

The *GPI* information will give other compensations that should be enacted at school. Refer to those and add them. Here are a few of the compensations and errors directly from the *GPI*.

Seeing too much[9]

Your children sometimes see more than we do. This interferes with the reading process. Reducing glare helps them. Find out if materials on colored

---

[8] Different states and school districts have different names for this formal conference each school year. The meeting refers to the educational planning meeting between school professionals and parents.
[9] From the *GPI* informational report

paper are easier to read. Certain colors may work better than others.

Top Neglect[10]

If written directions are not understood, this may be due to top neglect. Your children may not see the top of a page. These errors should not count. Point out the errors to your children. Have the teacher grade the assignment according to the way your children did the paper and then have them re-evaluated orally following the directions correctly.

Searching difficulty[11]

Finding words in lists (even alphabetical), hidden in searches, scrambled, and the like may be difficult for your children. They may need help finding words in glossaries, encyclopedias, dictionaries, and matching lists. Have another student help them find the entries. Avoid using word finds if they spend a great deal of time trying to find the words. Substitute

---

[10] From the *GPI* informational report. See Appendix B for information.
[11] Ibid.

other activities that are more educationally appropriate for them.

Miscounting[12]

Because of the serious visual distortion, your children may have difficulty counting. The difficulty is probably due to items seeming to split into more than one item or items combining. Do not expect accurate counting unless they are guided carefully.

Be sure to add all the specific compensations from your children's results of the *GPI* to their educational plan for the school year. The next chapter contains other general issues in learning how to read and how to overcome them. These reading issues are not related to the distortion from the processing errors, but are common problems that many students encounter.

---

[12] Ibid. See Appendix B for information.

Chapter 3

Additional Reading Problems and Solutions

In addition to the physical visual distortions listed in Chapter Two, your children may have common reading issues. In this chapter, we identify these common reading issues not related to the visual distortion. These problems can aggravate the visual distortion and need to be treated along with the distortion.

In this chapter, we discuss the following:

- Analysis of why people do not read
- Difficulties embedded in the reading process
- Other issues
- Conclusions for the educational plan

Analysis of why people do not read

As you work toward correcting your children's reading problems caused by visual distortions (Chapter 2), you need to analyze possible additional sources for their reading problems. The additional general categories of reading problems that I found are maturational lag, developmental misunderstanding, emotional difficulties, nutritional needs, and social issues.

Because these common issues affect reading along with the visual distortion, they must be part of the solution for correcting your children's reading problems. The additional categories of reading problems are not part of the visual processing disability. Fortunately, through time, they *will* correct themselves if appropriate compensation for them is made. These issues may have added to your children's reading confusion. The corrections for these problems should be included in their educational plan.

Maturational lag

Maturational lag is when the abilities to focus on print, remember letters and sounds, have fine motor control to write answers, and develop classroom behaviors appear later than they do with their peers. As your children mature, they develop these skills; therefore, this problem is the easiest and also the hardest to correct. Your children may grow slower than others. They will eventually have the ability to read. The major correction is to wait for the abilities to mature. This is the easy part of the correction. Waiting, however, means that your children will fall behind their peers educationally in all of their subjects, not just in reading. This is the part of correction we address.

While waiting for your children to mature, you need to maintain information input for them so that they do not fall behind their peers. They will eventually learn how to read. In the meantime, they need to keep learning subject material. They can continue to learn if others read to them and help them get information. Their family, volunteers, and peers are great resources for help with reading until they learn to read themselves.

Your family can help by using your children's interests. These interests become the topics that are read to them. They will rarely read for fun when reading is not fun. They will learn to read when they want to know something. This process is different from students who do not have maturational lag. Instead of funny and fanciful stories, your children will tend to learn to read through informational reading. After they get meaning from the printed page, they will learn to use reading for entertainment. Remember that *reading for fun does not work when reading is not fun.*

At school, volunteers can read to your children. They can also help with reading at home. Your children's reading problems create homework problems that could continue for years. Having volunteers help with homework can save your family from incredible stress.

Other students can also read to your children. These can be students in the same class or older students. Older students can use the reading as an opportunity for reviewing material they need to review.

Maturational lags will eventually self-correct; however, the problems that your children have as a result of not reading must be dealt with. When your children keep up with their peers through reading assistance, they will be able to continue in normal classes. If compensations for the reading problems are not made, they will fall farther and farther behind. Volunteers, peers, and family members can read to them to maintain their education.

Developmental misunderstanding

Your children may not understand what reading is. They may not understand what they are trying to do during the reading process. They need to learn that words are on the page. You can help them understand this by putting their own words onto a page. You can describe reading as finding out what someone wanted to say to them. You can call it, "Talking on paper." You start this process by having your children describe what they see. You write down what they say as they say it. Then you have them read it back to you. They may be able to read very quickly after they understand what reading actually is.

When volunteers, family, and peers read, your children learn that sentences and words are on the page. However, when volunteers are not available, you can use recordings of what needs to be read. Recordings are available through Learning Partners for children fifth grade and above. When you introduce recordings, be sure to sit with your children to show them how to use the recordings.

In addition, you can use apps which read material to your children. As technology advances, more and more services are available for your children. Be sure to use any available resource to help your children enjoy and use the printed page. Remember that their best resource is a real person reading with them.

Another method that has been used to assist readers is video recordings of books. The recordings have the words printed on the screen. Usually, these have not worked well because your children may ignore the words and just listen to the audio.

You can teach a foreign language to your children. I recommend using a language that is part of your children's heritage. We have noticed that students who have struggled with English performed very well as they learned foreign languages! Probably their struggles with English helped them learn a new language. Encourage your children if they want to learn a new language.

When your children do not understand what is happening with the reading process, they fail to read. They may think that they need to memorize the words. They may be quite mystified by the printed page. Once they understand that reading is talking on paper, they will quickly adapt to the process.

In summary, when you write your children's actual words, you can read the words back to them. Next you have them read the words. Through this process, they will learn that *reading is talking on paper*. You can encourage them to write notes, so that they can practice talking to others on paper. A number of these suggestions were mentioned in the previous chapter. The next chapter on writing will go deeper into ways to encourage their writing.

Two additional ideas to try came from talking with professionals in many fields. I explained how Braille had worked to engage my daughter in reading. As we brainstormed ideas of ways to help families, these professionals suggested using Morse code and sign language to help teach reading. I have not tried these, but offer them to you as possibilities for helping your children learn how to read. Contact me when you find additional ways to help your children be successful. I will add your ideas to the increasing information regarding successful ways to overcome processing problems.

Emotional difficulties

When your children learn how to read, they are quite young. They are still reliant on their caregivers. They may feel uncomfortable when they are working within the strange surroundings of school. At home, be careful to read in an environment that is welcoming and safe for them. When you volunteer at school, you are also bridging the gap between home and school and helping to make school a safer place for your children.

Your children may need to learn to control their emotions. They may need a place to act out safely. They may need to be able to move around frequently. They may need to stand while you read together rather than sit still. The movement allows them to divert their emotional overstimulation into physical activities. My grandson will sometimes read sitting upside down. Let your children try any way that they feel comfortable as long as they keep on reading.

Even when your children are older, they may need similar accommodations. Allowing them freedom to walk around in the room as you read and to use the bathroom as needed helps your children release emotional tensions. Allowing freedom of movement within boundaries can help your children meet their emotional issues.

If your children have extreme emotional problems, they will need professional assistance to be comfortable in the classroom setting. These suggestions are for children who are uncomfortable about learning because they have been marginally successful or unsuccessful.

Your children may be uncomfortable because they miss their family. Volunteer at school to help your children feel more comfortable. Tell your children's teacher what helps them feel more comfortable. View your study places at home through your children's eyes to create the most successful environment possible for them. By reducing stress from external sources, you can help your children focus on learning and reading.

Nutritional needs

Nutritional needs vary from person to person. When your children's physical needs are met, they will function cognitively. If they are hungry, they need food. Your children may not be able to go four hours without food. You can find out their eating patterns at home. A doctor would need to verify that your children need snacks during school time.

For example, I helped a young mother learn math. When I brought food, she ate hungrily. She jumped at the chance to get food. She was very tiny, but she ate constantly. When she ate, she was able to think and reason. When she did not eat, she was sluggish and unable to read, write, or think.

Another student crashed when he came in from afternoon recess. If he ate, he stabilized. When he did not eat, at the end of the day, he could not control himself. When he ate frequently, he did not crash and made it through the afternoon easily. Control issues disappeared when his physical need for food was met.

These examples demonstrate the importance of responding to your children's nutritional needs – even at school. They may need to eat more frequently than is scheduled during the school day. They may need to snack all day. Be sure to check with their doctor if you suspect they need to eat more frequently at school. Hunger will keep them from being able to concentrate on the school tasks.

Physical needs of students

Another issue that can affect your children is going to the bathroom. They may need to have privacy to use the bathroom. They may need to use the bathroom while the other children are not around. When they are allowed to use the bathroom during class time, they can relieve themselves. As a result, they will do much better in school.

Be sure they do not solve the bathroom problem by not drinking at school. This can create health problems throughout life. Encourage your children to get their fluids and have access to the bathroom as needed.

Physical needs are critical to learning. Your children cannot learn when they have unmet physical needs. Their physical needs must be met through adequate breaks for food, drinks, or the bathroom.

Above (in Emotional difficulties) we discussed viewing the learning environment from a comfort perspective to help you decide how a study place feels to your children. Reading also requires a comfortable setting. You can ask these questions to be sure you have the best possible location:

- Where do you read with your children?

- Do your children's reading places fit their needs?
- Do your children need changes in the place where you read and study?
- Have you considered all five senses?
    - Smell: close to memory centers
    - Taste: comfort and security
    - Feel: stuffed animals and soft items
    - Sight: clean and not over stimulated
    - Sounds: ambient noise distracters

Where do you read? You choose a comfortable spot. If you sit at a desk, even one your size and try to read, you will soon be squirming and uncomfortable. In the same way, you must provide comfortable seating for both of you at reading times. When you read, feel free to sit on your sofa. Ask your children to suggest reading places. When they are involved in creating their surroundings, they will also be more comfortable reading.

Have you considered all five senses? Some children are sensitive in one sense and not another. Your children can be distracted if a sensitive sense receives negative input.

Smell: close to memory centers

Smells can be helpful in remembering. Since the smell center is next to the memory center of the brain, smells can activate your children's memory. For example, when they read about Thanksgiving, they may almost smell the turkey roasting. Religious settings may be comforting because of peace offered, but also because of the smell of candles. The smell of baking and cooking in your home is also welcoming.

You can ask your children about their favorite smells. You also need to ask them about smells that bother them. You can help your children remember school work by bringing smells into the room that help them feel good. Be careful to avoid smells that are too powerful. When smells are too powerful, your children may focus on the smells rather than the information. This defeats the purpose of enhancing the memory through smells. Also, avoid any smells that your children do not like since these would be repulsive and prevent their memory from enjoying the information and remembering it.

Taste: comfort and security

The expression "comfort foods" demonstrates this concept. Your children need healthy snacks when they are hungry. They can experience severe pain when they are hungry. Because of concern for overweight, you must be careful to watch that you do not encourage too much eating; however, when your children munch on healthy snacks, they will relax and remember why and what they are studying.

Feel: stuffed animals and soft items

Your children may feel their surroundings more than others. You may notice that they are uncomfortable sitting for very long. A cushion on a chair can help them concentrate on schoolwork. Let them snuggle a stuffed animal to soothe them during study time.

Sight: clean and not over stimulated color!

You can use visual input to help your children remember. One of the best ways to enhance visual input is to change it often. Rather than placing all the visual items for a lesson out on a table, you can put a single item out and change it when needed. As you use items, place them into play centers for your children to use after you finish.

Some rooms are extremely busy rooms. The visual input can be distracting for your children because of their visual problems. They may see more than others and may be easily distracted by items floating from the ceiling and peering at them from every part of the room. You can use good decorating sense in your children's learning areas, just as you do in other rooms of your home.

Sounds: ambient noise distracters

You may be able to ignore background sounds, such as light fixtures, pages turning, pencils scratching paper, heart beats, and the like, no matter where you are. You may say that the world could fall apart around certain people, and they would not notice; however, your children may be distracted by every sound, no matter how soft. Whatever you can do to minimize noise in the learning environment will help your children learn better.

Carpeting or area rugs can help absorb sounds. Curtains on windows help reduce sound. Sounds can be muffled when they cannot be removed. Sound barriers can be used around noisy equipment.

Social issues

Your children may not like school. They may feel as if no one likes them. They seem to be all right at school, but report to you that they do not like school. Their reading problems can make them feel inferior to other students. Encourage relationships with other students in their classes as well as participation in activities that your children enjoy, for example, sports, music, art, dance, or drama.

As your children become more successful, their confidence will grow, and they will form more friendships. As they relax, these problems will disappear.

In the above, you can see how additional issues beyond visual distortions can also affect learning. These were maturational lag, developmental misunderstanding, emotional difficulties, nutritional needs, and social issues. When processing problems are also present, treating these additional issues is even more critical. Your children will need all the support you can give them in overcoming all areas of learning interference.

Difficulties embedded in the reading process

In addition to the above issues, the reading process itself can create problems. Your children will learn to read silently and to read orally. When your children first learn to read, they spend a greater proportion of reading time reading orally rather than silently. This oral process of reading has an auditory lag problem, phonics irregularities, and word calling that can affect reading. I describe these problems next.

Auditory lag

When children read out loud, between what your children see on the page and what they hear themselves say is a slight time lag. Since the lag is very slight, most children are not disturbed by it. Your children may be very perceptive and have difficulty reading aloud because they notice that what they are seeing does not match what they actually are hearing.

An example that is a similar slight time lag in processing is the lag when you sign your name on a computer signature screen at a store. What you are writing does not appear visually as fast as you physically write it. This minor lag can affect the way you sign. Most people's signatures are quite sloppy on the computer screen when compared with their signatures on paper.

Because your children can hear the slight lag between visual input and auditory output, they may have difficulty concentrating enough to read aloud. The disturbance is too annoying to let them think about what they are reading. As they read aloud more and more, they will become used to the lag and overcome this problem. Practice reading at home with them and talk about what they see and hear. Ask them if they notice the lag. If they do, explain it to them to help them overcome it. Keep reading with them to let them get used to the lag.

Phonics irregularities

A second issue in the reading process is the irregularity in the rules of phonics. An example of this is: **Fish** could be spelled **ghoti** if we used **gh** as in cough for the **f** ; **o** as the short **i** as in women, **ti** is the **sh** sound in nation. Therefore **ghoti** could spell **fish**. We could have a lot of problems seeing that. In a similar manner, the irregular spellings and changes in letter sounds affect your children's reading.

In addition, your children may be keenly aware of the problems with the rules of spelling and phonics. They cannot get past the irregularities. Actually pointing out the irregularities can help them learn to read. When they start to tell you what they see as problems with the rules, they can recognize that they are correct in their analyses of the "errors" in the rules. Then they can learn to use the rules and make the appropriate exceptions to them.

Remember, very young children have an enormous problem accepting exceptions to rules. The phonics and spelling irregularities can prevent your children from accepting the rules. They sometimes reject reading as impossible to understand. To help them accept reading, call the words that do not follow the rules **weird words**. Make a big deal about how they break the rules. Talk about how someone made a mistake a long time ago, and now we have to live with that mistake. Agree that the words are spelled wrong! We had to do this with my grandson who insisted that **bringed** should be used for **brought**!

Your children can learn to overcome the oral reading lag and the irregularities of phonics. They will need help recognizing the problems and accepting them. Once they have accepted them, they can work through the issues successfully.

Word calling

Another problem your children may have is word calling. They may read very accurately, but are disconnecting the reading from their consciousness. They are simply reading the words without understanding anything they are saying. They are calling out the words without forming a meaningful connection. They read perfectly out loud, but have no understanding of what they have read. This problem may be due to the reading lag. To correct for this problem, do the following:

Step One

Ask your children what they see when they read. When they are word calling, they will not be able to tell you that they see anything. Here are some of the answers that indicate word calling: *I see black*; *I see white*; *I see nothing*; or *huh*?

If your children indicate that they are not seeing anything as they read, do Step Two.

Step Two

- Tell your children that when you read, you visualize the activities and imagine what happens in the book or story.
- Next, have your children look around them and describe something in the area.
- As they are telling you what they see, write down their descriptions in their exact words.
- Tell them you wrote what they said, and check if they can read their own words.
- Ask them what they saw when they read. They may be able to see that what they are reading was what they just said. They may, however, not recognize their own words and still **see** black, white, nothing, or be as confused as before.
- If they **see** what they described, you will notice a flash of recognition on their faces.

Do this again to be sure they are really seeing what is written. Then write something to them and see if they can see what you said. If they can, you have broken the word calling. Go on to other reading. If they still cannot see anything while reading, continue to Step Three.

Step Three
- Read their words to them as they close their eyes.
- Ask them what they *see*.
- If they see the same as what their words described, ask *them* to read the words.
- Some students will suddenly be able to read and see effectively from this point on. If not...
- Explain that the words are what they described and have them read the words again. Ask them to try to let the words help them see what they were describing.

After this exercise, your children should be able to visualize and connect with their reading. In order to maintain the correction, write their words and have them read the words back on a daily basis. Also, have other people write letters to them. Have volunteers and family members write to them. As an added benefit, have them answer the notes and letters - writing practice!! Help your children to write their notes to others.

Other issues

In addition to the above suggestions for helping students learn to read, we have found the following to be helpful:

Give more assignments, not fewer

An analogy will help us understand why your children need more assignments and more practice since they have difficulties processing information. When you have a serious injury, you are given intensive therapy to help you recover from the injury. In the same way, since the reading problems are extremely serious, you cannot reduce reading practice. You must increase it. Practice must be carefully monitored so that your children do not harm themselves more. You should monitor that practice to be sure they are reading accurately.

Use alternative reading methods

Since you cannot be sure when your children's reading will become age-appropriate, you must provide additional reading assistance until your children can read independently at their grade level or above. Methods that were described above are critical. Peers can help with reading content area material. Peers can read words, sentences, and even sections of material. An extra benefit of peer assistance is that peers' grades improve as they assist your children. Older students can assist with the reading process. They can use the experience as an opportunity to review material as they adapt to their own processing problems. In addition, older students can be highly intelligent students who finish their work quickly. They will recognize that your children are also highly intelligent. This will give your children an opportunity to model the bright students' behaviors.

Your children will probably need many people to provide the reading assistance that is necessary. A third group of people that can assist with the extensive reading assistance that is needed is volunteers. Volunteers should be trained to help with reading. They need to read fast and accurately without giving answers. They do not need to be concerned with teaching reading. They need to be the accurate readers for your children.

Record reading assignments

The best way to record reading assignments is to audio and visually record actual people reading them out loud. Your children then see, as well as, hear the readers. They will tend to ignore the printed word when they use any recordings. As a result, whenever actual readers can be present, have people do the reading with them.

When volunteers, peers, and older students are not available and video recording is not possible, you can use audio recordings. These are much more difficult for your children. There is only the auditory input. Unfortunately, they can easily lose focus as they listen to them. Again, the best way to provide reading assistance is with a person actually reading with them.

Train for independent reading

The most important goal of all the adjustments is to help your children be able to read alone. One method that can be used is to spiral through material to review and to show them that they had learned the material. Spiraling is going back to the very first educational material and quickly reviewing it. Reviews are described below. In the spiraling method, all first grade material should be reviewed in as little as one to two days. As the material has more volume, the spiraling review will take a little longer.

Also, spiraling gives an opportunity to show your children how to use the compensations that are needed. To spiral material, your children will review material from kindergarten through their present grade level. Their memory of past school years is that they failed. By spiraling through the material, they will learn that they have successfully accomplished learning it.

Spiraling involves using questions at the end of chapters to review the material. Your children will learn how to find answers if they do not know them. Also, they learn how to check that answers they know are written correctly. Spiraling is a rapid review of social studies, science, language, reading, and mathematics. The usual time for spiraling varies from weeks to eighteen months. During spiraling, your children will review all the subjects from past years. They will also go through all the material for their present grade placement. They should spiral about one year above what they will see in their regular classroom. While they are spiraling, if possible they should *not* take the subjects in their regular classroom at school. The last step of spiraling is to catch up with missed assignments. Then they are ready to use their compensations as they return to regular education.

A major reason for spiraling is to teach your children that they can easily learn huge amounts of material. Also, they will learn that they have been successfully learning material, even though they may have received low grades the first time they went through the material.

Your children need reassurance that they actually do know how to read. They need practice learning how to check that what they are seeing is what is actually written. Spiraling offers them these opportunities. However, spiraling will not overcome years of difficulty. Your children will need assistance from tutors, volunteers, family members, and peers until they can read accurately on their own. This can take years of assistance from others.

Teach reading from long vowels and weird words

Since your children do not have stable visual clues, they need to know about the irregularities in the spelling and phonics rules. They are processing so much distortion that whenever you can give them assistance in understanding irregularities, they are able to process better.

Vowel sounds are quite irregular. Some reading series begin by teaching the many forms for long vowels. Your children can depend on the long vowels saying their names. They are able to remember the many spellings (probably because that's the way the letters present themselves to them, anyway). Using long vowel sounds seems to help with spelling, also.

When editors of reading programs used just long vowels, they also used the concept of words that did not fit the rules (*the, there, what, was, where*, etc.). You can teach these irregular words to your children. Earlier we called these words *weird words*. They do not follow the rules.

Use headings and titles

One reason your children ignore titles and headings is because then they are reading without context. They may also ignore them because of top neglect. Top neglect is a visual problem that means they do not see information at the top of the page. Regardless of the reason that your children are not reading headings and titles, they need instruction and reading assistance to learn to use these important features effectively. Otherwise, they miss the keys to main ideas in selections and begin reading without the focus of the headings and titles.

Use glossaries

Alphabetical listings are very difficult to use when your children have visual distortions. A story about two adult students gives an example of the difficulty of using a glossary. The two were determined to look up their definitions in biology without assistance. They were sure they could help each other. This is what happened.

Greg: What word am I looking up?

Sara: Biosphere

Greg: Thanks. A, c, d, e. I went past it. Ok, now I am in the b's. What was the word, again?

Sara: Just a minute, I have to check. I think it was biology.

Oh, no, wait, it was botany. No, that is not right. Here it is, ecosystem.

Greg: Great! I am in the wrong place. F, g, h, i... What was the word, please? What letter does it start with?

As the two struggled, others offered to help. The offers were refused until, after over 15 minutes, the two were able to accept help in finding their first definition.

This example is a true story. It demonstrates several problems that your children may have:

- They forget the word that they are looking up.
- They cannot remember the alphabetical order.
- They cannot remember the spellings.
- They are determined to do their work independently.

This example shows how desperately your children need help finding entries in glossaries, indices, and the like. You can have peers and volunteers find the words quickly and accurately for your children at school. Searching for words is a task that is much easier on the computer. However, getting the words typed in accurately is a major problem. Your children will still need help with finding the words on the computer.

During spiraling, demonstrate how to answer questions. Guide your children until they find all the correct answers. Finally, find index and glossary entries for your children. Help them answer 100% accurately!!

Conclusions for the educational plan[13]

Reading is a fundamental skill for learning. Your children may have difficulty learning how to read because of visual distortions, maturational lag, developmental misunderstanding, emotional difficulties, nutritional needs, social issues, and the reading process itself. Each area must be carefully examined. All needed adjustments and compensations must be made so that your children can effectively learn and grow educationally.

---

[13] The meeting refers to the educational planning meeting between school professionals and parents.

Chapter 4
Suggestions for Writing Accurately

In my research, writing disruption was the processing problem that I most frequently observed. When your children write, they may not write as they intend and are quite unaware that they are miswriting. When they get an assignment back, they can be extremely frustrated by their errors. This chapter gives you the adaptations and compensations for writing so that you can help your children demonstrate their ability through writing. We will discuss:

- The physical nature of writing problems
- Alternate methods of recording information
- The second phase of writing
- Checking for specific writing errors
- Using the Geiman Method: a case study
- What to do at the instructional planning meeting

The physical nature of writing problems

When you watch your children write, you may see that they are having difficulty writing. They may write one letter for another. They may skip a word. They may write the wrong word. They may forget how to write a letter. They may write a letter twice. They may write a word twice. They may forget how to spell words. They may forget what they were trying to write. All of these errors and more can be checked with the *General Processing Inventory (GPI)*. Their specific errors are then listed for them and you. The error corrections are also listed. These corrections are very important for your children. They could be as impaired as a person who is paralyzed.

In fact, I ran a study with a paralyzed person and a person who has these writing errors. The person with the writing errors wrote slower than the person who was documented as 100% paralyzed. The person with processing errors not only was much slower, but also had many more errors. The paralyzed person was slow, but not as slow as the person with processing problems. He had no errors. Your children may not look as if they need help, but indeed they do.

Alternate methods of recording information

At the beginning of training, you will do a lot of writing for your children. As you and your children progress through the training period, you will do less and less writing until you are phased out completely. You may end up as an editor after training is completed. The following is what you should do during training.

Have your children tell you what to write. If they have an assignment that can be completed on a computer, do the writing on the computer. If not, write exactly what they say onto the assignment. Have them tell you when they want a capital letter, comma, period, or question mark after you have written the words. Write in pencil, so that you can make changes as they request them. Write exactly as they say it. Do not ask them questions or interrupt their thought process. Let them guide your writing of their thoughts. In fact, you may use a recorder and then type or write from that recording. Finally, both of you will make corrections to your transcription of their actual words as described above. Always have your children present and telling you what to write while you type or write – even when you transcribe an audio or audio/visual recording of their words.

The goal of this first phase of writing is to put your children's thoughts on paper. Your children use you as a scribe possibly with a recorder. Your children are not writing anything – yet. As soon as the written recording of their thoughts is completed, read the material with your children. Depending on their reading ability, you may have to read it, or you may be able to have them read some of it. Read exactly what is written. As you read the material together and they find errors, you correct the writing immediately. They should interrupt you whenever they hear an error. Now they should add the punctuation and capitalization, too.

Read the writing at least three times together. Each time, your children should hear and recognize their own errors, but you should correct them. When you have finished editing three times, look at the material again. If there are still errors that you see, point them out to your children and put editing marks for the errors. Have them do these corrections.

The second phase of writing

Now your children start the writing process. Remind them that when they were dictating to you, you could not keep up with their speech. They may also have noticed that their speech was not keeping up with their thoughts. These lags are part of the reason they have difficulty writing. They have to remember what they want to say, how to spell it, in what order to place the letters and words, and how to punctuate. Writing is very complex.

See if they write better on a computer or on paper. Use the way that they are the fastest. Do not worry about accuracy while they are writing. They will get many times to edit.

As soon as your children become unable to continue writing and are frustrated even slightly, ask if they want you to write. Follow their lead and let them continue to write if they wish. Let them know that you are ready to write again at their request. After you or they write the entire assignment or a section of it, you both start the editing again. Read exactly what they wrote on the paper. When they hear an error, correct it immediately. After a few edits, you will point out any errors that you still see and have your children correct the errors.

During the training process, let your children guide who is writing and who is reading. If they are struggling, ask them if they want you to take over. Only let them struggle a few seconds before asking if they want your help. Immediately write when they request it. Respect their wishes if they want to try writing themselves. Edit with them so that they see the errors and learn about the editing process. Editing takes as long as, or longer, than the writing process.

Teaching your children the editing process will help them throughout their lives. One student organized an entire office to do editing like this with all the other employees. He received an award. Another person organized editing for professionals and developed writing programs for helping college students learn how to edit.

Editing writing is your children's key to successful writing. They will need to learn to use computer writing and recording of their thoughts so that they can get their ideas on paper accurately and quickly without forgetting what they wanted to write. You will probably be an editor for them for quite a while.

Checking for specific writing errors

When your children write, they have specific error patterns that were discovered through the *GPI*. They should practice looking for these errors as they edit. The list of errors may be too long to use all at once. Help them look for a single error first. Then as they practice editing, you can have them look for two errors as they edit. Then as they get better at editing, they can look for multiple errors. When they finish their edits, be sure to check for the other errors that were identified through the *GPI*.

As your children practice editing, they are learning the errors they should expect to see. They may improve their processing and may not. They need to learn what they do so that they can find their specific processing errors and correct them. They may need to wait for a few hours or even over night before they will be able to see their own errors. They should be encouraged that this is the way professional writers get their material polished. My editor brother, Bill, calls it "word-smithing." They should keep going over the material until it is smooth and polished. The more times they look at their writing, the better it gets.

Using the Geiman Method (a case study)

For ten weeks, I worked with a first grader. Before compensations, he took half an hour to partially complete one worksheet, and he could barely write a sentence. After the training he could write his own answers on worksheets that were age-appropriate. He still dictated longer passages of writing. When he wanted me to write answers on worksheets, he could give me the spellings of the words and not just the words. This took ten weeks of gradual transformation. After ten weeks of daily half-hour lessons, he could dictate a page of writing and do ten worksheets in half an hour. He still has a long way to go, but he no longer fusses and fumes about his work, either!

Your children will progress at their own rate. Allow them to be successful and to complete their work quickly. They will need your encouragement and assistance. This process can take up to 18 months to be fully completed.

What to do at the instructional planning meeting

Be sure all the *GPI* adjustments for writing that are suggested for teachers are included in your children's educational plan. Spelling words should be graded letter by letter. Written work should be done with peers and teachers in the same way as you are doing it at home.

In addition to the *GPI* teacher compensations, be sure that the personal, peer, and family compensations are included. At school, other students can be scribes and readers. This will help both your children and the other children. Using peers at school also helps your children get the care that is essential for them to be able to communicate accurately.

In chapters 5, 6, 7, and 8, I will discuss how writing will be adjusted in studying and homework, doing math, taking tests, and spelling. These four areas of the educational process are very dependent on the writing process. When the *GPI* writing compensations are enacted, your children's performance in all subject areas will improve dramatically.

Chapter 5

Studying and Homework

Since your children have serious problems, they may try to avoid homework. In this chapter, we will discuss how you can retrain your children so that they complete tasks when your children are fresh enough to do them well. Creating schedules for doing unpleasant tasks helps your children learn to do the tasks and do them well.

We will cover:

- Worst tasks first
- Rewards for completing tasks
- Scheduling the unpleasant
- Completing all tasks as directed
- Passing through four stages of learning when studying
- Identifying the stage necessary for a task and the level of study of the task
- Adaptations to be sure information is accurately recorded
- Sorting information to learn it
- Additional adaptations for studying
- Entering information into the educational plan

Worst tasks first

When your children come home from school, greet them and give them a snack and a few minutes to chat with you. After about fifteen minutes, sit down with your children and have work for yourself to do while you monitor their studying.

At first, you will be helping your children determine the worst assignment for them. Do that one first so that it is over. Help your children read directions and material that needs to be read before the assignment can be completed. When your children want to read, let them. Watch that they are getting the information accurately.

Remember to help your children select the worst assignment each day. On different days, the worst assignment may change as they get comfortable with certain school tasks. Let them help you select which task they are dreading that day. Then complete it and enjoy the other tasks.

One particular school task serves as an example of doing the worst or hardest first. Multiple choice questions are difficult because the answers are usually similar and without context. Instead of reading the question and then the answers, have your children do the worst task first and read all of the answers. Then have them read the question for that set of answers. Now have them tell why the answers are wrong. You may ask them if the wrong answers are silly or jokes. Make sure they try every answer before picking the correct answer. Doing the hardest part of the task first helps make the entire task easier and more accurate.

Rewards for completing tasks

When the first assignment is completed, you and your children can determine the reward for completing it. For example, I reward myself for completing tasks by playing a game on the computer.

Your children can help you draw up a list of rewards. Some days, they may want a snack. For other tasks, they may want a break; at other times, they may want to keep on with the next assignment, but they want to choose what that next assignment will be. Regardless, as your children complete each assignment, have an appropriate reward for completing the task.

Your children can learn to expect that studying and completing homework will result in good things. Be sure to keep the rewards healthy, short, inexpensive, and practical. Have a partial list of rewards prepared before you discuss rewards with your children. Let them choose the reward from your list of rewards.

Scheduling the unpleasant

At times, more than one, maybe even all, of the homework tasks will be quite unpleasant. Now you and your children will have to schedule the tasks. Set specific times to complete each task. In between the homework times, allow a break with an activity that your children choose. They may need to work on the difficult tasks with shorter easier assignments mixed in. They may need to take longer breaks and schedule the time for getting back to the homework after play time, supper time, or a short break. Keep the scheduled time.

While your children do their homework, have something to do that can keep you available nearby. I did crossword puzzles, read books of my own, did needlework, and the like. At times, I cooked and had my children stand at the counter with me while they wrote out their answers. Standing was a nice change of pace for them. Just be sure to keep the scheduled times for the tasks that are difficult. They need to see that homework can be over quickly and that the homework is their personal responsibility! The purpose for scheduling the unpleasant tasks is so that they have a full evening for other activities.

Completing all tasks as directed

Your children will sometimes want to complete a task without doing all of it or doing it without following all the directions. Stand firm in requiring that the homework is completed in the way that the directions said. Your children may have to work harder than other students to complete the homework, but that persistence will soon be seen as the norm for their work.

Passing through four stages of learning when studying

Your children pass through four stages of learning. In addition, due to the spiraling nature of the school curriculum, assignments will be at different stages of learning. These stages are introduction, development, mastery, and memorization.

At the **introductory stage,** concepts are given for the first time. Your children are expected to use that introduction to **develop** ideas in the next lessons or in following years. When they are able to perform skills and discuss concepts easily, they have **mastered** concepts. Finally, they have to remember or **memorize** the concepts to be able to integrate them into their lives and other topics for study.

Since learning in every stage except the **introductory stage** is dependent on the stages that have gone before it, your children must accurately learn material at every stage. They must have accurate input of information at all stages of learning. Reading material for them and checking that they have read material accurately are critical.

Introductory stage

When your children have never seen material before and need to master it, they will need to pass through all four stages of learning. First, **introduce** them to the concept. Let them page through the material and preview it. They should notice words and symbols that are new to them and keep track of those words. They need a pleasant introduction to help them want to go deeper into the concept. When they are ready, have them go to the developmental stage.

Developmental stage

As your children continue to study, they may get confused by the input of new material. Take time to clarify their questions. Let them go back over any material to refresh it, so they can continue with confidence.

During the developmental stage, they may become easily frustrated as they try to put the ideas together. They may struggle to remember the steps for procedures. They may want to quit.

Help your children pass through the frustration so that they can get to the next stage of mastery. In the developmental stage, they will almost understand the ideas and almost be able to answer questions about the material. Let them correct themselves and check their notes and hints as they pass through this stage. Let them be sure of their answers and help them check that they are receiving and interpreting information accurately.

Mastery stage

The light bulb goes on! At the mastery stage, you will see your children's facial expressions and attitude suddenly change as they understand material. This step is sometimes out of the blue. It means that your children have put the pieces of information together into a meaningful concept for them.

Many times, mastery is overlooked before going to the memorization phase. Be sure your children truly understand what they are doing before trying to remember it.

Memorization or maintenance stage

Not only do your children have to understand or master a concept, but they also must remember it to use it later and to answer questions about the concept. After they understand a concept, ask them about it until they can remember all the details of the concept. Now they should use memory aids to help them remember definitions of key words, steps of processes, differences and similarities of information, and the like. They will need to review consistently and accurately to be sure they maintain the concepts. Also, when they have to use a concept they learned in the past, have them review the concept to help them remember the details of it.

Identifying the stage necessary for a task and the level of study of the task

Some assignments are not intended to be memorized or remembered until later years. Be sure to clarify with your children's teachers what the purpose of an assignment is. If they are to be guided through the lesson, you can offer more help. If they are to demonstrate that they have mastered a concept, you will let them do the work with as little help as possible. Your children's teachers are the best people to let you know the purpose of an assignment. These will be introductory, developmental, mastery, and maintenance, too.

Follow the compensations that are given in the *GPI* when you do not know what to do to help. These are necessary adjustments to make as your children do their homework and studies.

Adaptations to be sure information is accurately recorded

When your children are completing assignments, check their work to be sure they are answering as they intend. Look at the material using the check list from the *GPI* to adjust for any additional writing issues they may have.

When you are asked to record information for them, be sure to be true to their words and use their actual words and expressions. Resist the temptation to edit their work to make them look better. They need to edit their own work. Be sure that they actually understand their own errors and are learning from the editing process.

Here is a story to show you how they could do editing without learning from the process:

My daughter learned that she could accept the changes that her family would make on a computer document. She stopped asking me to help her because she could get someone else to enter the corrections into the computer draft of her work. Then she clicked the key for accept changes and was done. (Until I found out!)

Sorting information to learn it

While your children are learning a concept and when they are working on remembering it, they should use sorting to help them organize the material. For example, if they were studying about a topic such as weather, they could find all the words that are descriptions of precipitation. Then they could evaluate the words for their differences. First they would group the words to chunk the material, and then they would clarify each term by its uniqueness. In their precipitation list, they may have: *rain, hail, snow, sleet, dew, frost*.

Next they would separate the terms by several factors, such as temperature, consistency of the precipitation, or time of the day when the precipitation occurs.

They could list the terms in a chart:

Precipitation	Temperature	Consistency	Time of day
Rain	Above 32°	Liquid	Any
Dew	Above 32°	Liquid	Night and sunrise
Frost	Below 32°	Solid	During the night and noticed at sunrise
Sleet	Around 32°	Solid/liquid	Any
Hail	Usually above 32°	Solid	Any
Snow	Usually below 32°	Solid	Any

They do not need to make the chart neat. They can draw it by hand. If you have access to a computer, though, they can give you the information. You can enter it in a table as above. As they get used to the process, let them type information into the table themselves. Help them as needed.

Additional adaptations for studying

Your children's reports from the *GPI* will list many additional adaptations that they need. You may need to write answers that they dictate. You may need to have a CD player, computer, or smart phone to help them hear recorded material. They may need help learning how to sort material so that they can remember it. You may have to quiz them and play memory games with them to prepare for quizzes and tests.

Entering information into the educational plan

Be sure to use all the compensations that are listed for your children in the results of the *GPI*. These compensations are critical and vital to their success. The *GPI* adaptations must be used to help your children learn best. They are not optional.

Chapter 6

Math

There are only four operations in basic arithmetic: addition, subtraction, multiplication, and division. There are only a few types of real numbers, including counting, whole, integers, fraction forms, and irrationals. However, the combinations of these numbers can be overwhelming to your children. You can help them see the patterns in the numbers that will make math easier. Looking for patterns can help them learn to enjoy math.

In this chapter, we discuss:

- How physical processing problems affect learning math
- Recycling concepts for meaning
- Applying concepts to real life
- Asking questions for meaning
- Completing assignments (homework four steps)
- Using an assignment notebook
- Additional math ideas
- Information for the educational plan

How physical processing problems affect learning math

The six physical problems identified by the *General Processing Inventory (GPI),* affect math processing. In addition, the symbols of math are not checked with most computer spell and grammar checkers. Your children are on their own to find their errors. Following all the compensations from the *GPI* is critical in math. The visual, writing, auditory, speech, and memory retrieval problems make learning math a very difficult process. You will need to assist your children until they can look for, find, and correct their own processing errors.

The symbols of math are an additional processing problem. Your children may not notice the difference between the four operation signs (*+, -, ×, ÷*). They may not be able to process the abbreviations accurately; for example: *mi., m, mm, min.,* and *ml* may all seem the same to them. You will notice that they are able to do their math at home accurately, but have difficulty doing it at school. The added noise of the classroom may make their processing disrupt even more at school.

Because of the visual distortion, your children may avoid reading directions and assume that they know what to do with a set of problems. They will need help learning to read all the material of a word problem and the directions, as well. Help them organize the material so that they can use it to answer the question or questions of the problem.

Writing answers accurately may create issues, too. They may miscopy problems and answers. They may reverse the order of the digits in a number. They may write a previous number or answer. They will need help to edit their written work.

Your children may forget the four hundred basic facts as they work their math problems. With the help of students who could not remember the math facts, I wrote a set of eight booklets to organize the math facts into patterns to help your children to remember them.[14]

In class, your children may say the wrong words as they answer questions. You may notice this at home, as well. They will not recognize that they have said the wrong number or word. They will be quite frustrated when they are misunderstood.

All of the misprocessing issues need to be addressed. The compensations for them are critical so that your children can demonstrate their understanding of the math concepts. In math grading, teachers will not have context, as

---

[14] Available from the author. See Appendix B.

they do with words, to help them see that your children truly did learn their material.

Recycling concepts for meaning

Recycling means to quickly review material from past years. Recycling is critical because math concepts are built on past knowledge. Your children will need to know all the information from past lessons. You can review this information by using the chapter reviews from the books. If your children can easily answer all the questions, go on to the next chapter. If they have difficulty with a problem, review the section in that chapter that teaches the concept. Do as many problems as they need to feel comfortable about the concept and process. Be sure they can answer the problems with no clues or help.

While your children are reviewing the concepts, be sure they can answer all the 200 addition and subtraction facts. If they cannot, use the Geiman pattern reviews of the facts.[15] When they start the multiplication and division reviews, use the Geiman pattern reviews, too, to make sure they know all 200 multiplication and division facts.

---

[15] Available from the author. See Appendix B.

In addition, have your children review operations with decimals, fractions, and signed numbers to be sure they can use all four operations with these different types of numbers. Fractions are reviewed in the Geiman fact books.

Also, make sure your children review the vocabulary words that are given in each chapter. These words are critical for your children's success. The two of you can use index cards to make flash cards of these words. Your children should be able to describe what each word means and give an example of the word. For example, a fraction can be a part of a whole number; 1/3 is a fraction. Be sure to use the definitions that are given in the review material. Then write the definitions in your children's words to be certain they understand what each definition means.

Applying concepts to real life

When you are reviewing math with your children, be sure to check for understanding. For example, relate the fractions to the measuring cups in your kitchen. Let your children fill the 1/3 cup and pour it carefully into a whole cup. They can experience that 3 of the 1/3 cups fill the whole cup. Do the same with 1/4, 1/2, and 1/8 cups.

When you are showing them the addition facts, have them adding things around your home. Have them add together how many plates to put on the table. For example, if there are three children and one grandmother and two parents, they would add 3 + 1 + 2. Show them how you use subtraction, too. Spending money or giving them money to spend for school supplies or clothes will help them learn about subtraction and budgeting.

Asking questions for meaning

While your children are reviewing the math, you may notice that they can do some processes, but have no idea what they are doing or why. Zimbardo, a psychologist who studied learning, discovered that children need to repeat an idea 10,000 times if it is meaningless. Your children do not have the time to repeat meaningless material. Be sure they understand what they are doing and why they are doing it. You can ask your teachers for help describing what is happening and why. Many times, they will have to think about the answers to those questions because math has been taught in very meaningless ways at times.

Get comfortable with hearing, "I don't know, but we will find out." Other resource people for asking questions are college mathematics professors or math education professors. They think about questions like these as part of their careers.

Completing assignments (homework four steps)

When your children miss just one assignment, their grades drop tremendously. This is the single most important fact that will help your children get released from their past failures in math. Your children must complete every homework assignment and turn each one in on time. They cannot afford to have late or missing assignments. In this section, we discuss adaptations to be sure that

- All homework is completed
- All completed homework is turned in on time
- Homework is done correctly (following directions)
- Homework is the right assignment (problems, questions, and pages)

All homework is completed

When your children miss just one homework assignment, this is what happens. If they had 100% on four assignments for the week and missed the fifth, they will have 100 + 100 + 100 + 100 + 0 = 400. Instead of earning the A as they thought they had, they barely earn a B. This is because the 400 is divided by the five grades that should have been completed $400 \div 5 = 80$, and their percentage goes to 80%. If they had a single item wrong on any of those four assignments, their grades drop into the 70s, and they earned a C. They must complete every assignment and do it to 100% accuracy. Then if they inadvertently miss an assignment, they still are in the B range.

All completed homework is turned in on time

Some teachers give late assignments a deduction. The first late day, 100% becomes 90%, the second late day, it becomes 80%, the third late day it becomes 70%, and the fourth late day, it is 60%. Your children cannot afford these deductions. They must turn in their work on time to avoid any penalties.

Even when teachers do not give late penalties, your children still have problems if they turn in their homework late. For example, the assignment can get lost by the teacher when your children's assignments are turned in after the others are already graded and turned back. One piece of paper is easy to lose in the many papers that a teacher receives. To avoid having to do the homework again, make copies if your children turn in any late assignments.

The biggest problem that your children have when they turn in late assignments is that they are removed from the teaching that went along with the assignment. They may not remember what the directions were. They may not remember what they were supposed to do in terms of the process. They no longer may remember the examples that the teacher did. They will probably forget the classroom activities that were associated with the assignment. Turning homework in on time is essential.

Homework is done correctly (following directions)

Many times the reason your children's performance is not acceptable is because they did the wrong thing with the material. The teacher has asked them to underline answers, and they circled them. They were to select three answers and they selected only two. Help your children read the directions before they start their assignments. Make sure they follow them exactly!

Also, have them check over the work that they do. Have your children check the addition, subtraction, multiplication, and division signs to be sure they did the correct operation. They should also check that they answered the facts correctly, for example, writing $3 + 4 = 7$. In addition, have them check their own specific list of *GPI* errors to correct for them.

Homework is the right assignment (problems, pages, or chapters)

Sometimes your children may hide their homework and say they did not do it when they do the wrong assignment. Have them turn in the work, even when they did the wrong page, problems, or chapter. This is a common error that they will have to check for every day. Be sure their assignments are being initialed by the teacher or a student who is reliable. Your children may be embarrassed that they did the wrong assignment and will hide that fact from their teachers. Make sure that the teacher is aware that this could happen.

Using an assignment notebook

If you decide to have your children use an assignment notebook, buy several at the beginning of the school year. You will probably need to buy more as the year passes. I recommend using a single sheet of paper each week that each teacher initials. The paper can be for a week, but may need to be replaced when it is lost. The purpose for the teacher's initials is to be sure that assignments are accurately and completely recorded.

Additional math ideas

Review the information from the *GPI* for additional ideas to help your children review mathematics. Mathematics learning is critical information for many careers. Math is definitely for girls and boys. Your children must use all the adaptations to be sure that they can succeed in math.

Information for the educational plan[16]

All the compensations that are listed for your children from the *GPI* results should be included in their educational plans. If you can avoid percentages of performance, do that. Instead include the actual methods that will be essential for your children to learn appropriately. Using these methods of checking for assignments, reading tests, making sure the correct numbers are written, and reviewing past material will ensure that your children have every opportunity to succeed in mathematical learning.

---

[16] Different states and school districts have different names for this formal conference each school year. The meeting refers to the educational planning meeting between school professionals and parents.

Chapter 7

Taking Tests

Taking tests is an activity that takes place at school, but you can prepare your children so that taking tests becomes easier. Refer to their compensations from the *General Processing Inventory (GPI)*. We will cover:

- Physical processing issues
- Test taking adaptations: Before the test, during the test, after the test
- Additional compensations
- Information for the formal educational process

Physical processing issues

The symptoms of writing, hearing, speaking, reading, and retrieval from memory all impact your children's performance on tests. Be sure that they are well aware of how they can avoid, get around, and compensate for their identified errors before they take their tests. The compensations that are listed for them in the *GPI* will make the difference in their being able to demonstrate their true ability or being tested on their disability.

The physical issues affect them in these ways:

- Writing misprocessing affects the accuracy of their written answers.
- Hearing problems interfere with understanding oral directions during the test.
- Speaking issues prevent them from asking appropriate questions which they need to have answered during the test.
- Reading irregularities distort the questions and written directions of the test.
- Retrieval glitches hide their true ability as they are unable to retrieve information.

Since these distortions affect test taking, your children need all compensations to be in place so that their true ability can be demonstrated as they take tests.

Test taking adaptations:
Before the test
Learn to relax

When your children begin to study, they may begin to show signs of stress. Watch them to see if they are tense. Teach them to recognize that they have tensed up. Then show them basic relaxation techniques to help them while they study with you and when they are at school taking the test.

Here are a few ideas that have worked well with many students. 1) Teach them to breathe in and out very slowly. When they feel the tension is gone, they can continue to study. 2) Next, teach them to start thinking about their feet and feel them. Then they should let their feet go limp - like a rag doll. Go up through their lower legs, upper legs, lower torso, upper torso, shoulders, neck, jaw, cheeks, and forehead. When they have relaxed, they may study again. Feel free to add additional relaxation techniques as they need them.

Use memory aids

As your children review material, they should do so in chunks of material that go together. They should pick small enough chunks so that they can easily recall what they are learning. As they learn a new chunk of material, they refresh and review the other chunks of material that they have learned.

Help your children check that they have remembered all steps correctly and completely. Compliment your children when they remember. Quickly and gently give them information when they forget. Have them continue to review until they know that they remembered all the material.

Your children should repeat material until it is 100% accurately repeated. Continue to review and add new material in small chunks. Help your children select the important information. Some children select the wrong information, for example, they remember that George Washington is wearing a red cummerbund in a picture in the book instead of remembering that he was a general of the army and the first president.

Keep information handy (e.g. cards)

Definitions are usually on tests. You can copy definitions with a copier or by hand. Put the information on cards. You can copy the information twice so that you can play matching games with your children to help them remember the material. Start with the five items that are most difficult for them. Add items as they remember the definitions.

You can also play board games and use the material from the subjects they are studying as their questions. For example, play Trivial Pursuit or Jeopardy. Play memory games with them. Keep the activities real games and fun. When they are relaxed, they will remember and be able to retrieve material easier.

Review daily

You can review material with your children as you are riding in the car or on the bus. As you review, remind your children that the reason you are reviewing is because everyone forgets over half of what they learn. Keeping the material fresh and reviewed is important. Expect that there will be a few items that will be forgotten and refresh them.

Your children should continue to review until the actual test is handed to them. They should continue to review on the way to school, between other classes, and as the test is being handed out to others. They should put away the review materials just before they receive the test.

Use spaced practice

Spaced practice means that your children should review with time in between different review sessions. They will remember material better if they spend short (no longer than an hour) periods of review time that are separated by several hours. They should review on more than one day to get the most benefit from the reviews.

Study for forever and for understanding

Your children should review the material thinking that they will need to know it for the rest of their lives, not just for the test. They will remember the material easier when they understand what they are learning and why they are learning it. Their studying should be related to goals that they make for themselves. They should help determine when and how long to study.

Here are a few other general processes for learning and reviewing material. Use different memory methods, for example, webbing, multiple types of presentations of the material, and rehearsal can all be used with over learning.

Webbing

When learning material, have your children write down all the ideas that go with the concept. Use a paper and write the ideas like a giant spider web to see how they connect.

Multiple types of presentations of the material

When learning a process, such as division in math, use different models and presentations of ideas so that they complement each other. For example, draw a diagram, use counters, and make a chart for the same problem so that your children see it in more than one way. These multiple ways of looking at a problem will give them multiple ways to access their memory when they need to remember the material.

Use models, actual objects, pictures, or drawings to help your children understand new and review material before they attempt to remember it. While they are using the models, have them record their observations so that they see the connection between the models and the words that describe the activity. When they need to memorize, use memory aids, such as poems, colors, songs, smells, first letter phrases, numbering, location hooks, or sorting to help them remember the material.

Rehearsal and over learning

Your children should keep reviewing material as they add new material. Until the test begins, your children should continue to review the material. They should put away the review material just before they take the copy of the test.

Sorting

Look for similarities and differences in material that needs to be memorized.

To summarize the preparation process:

- Have accurate input

- Use shaping steps
- Over learn
- Complete the stages of learning (introduction, development, mastery, memorization)
- Review, review, review
- Use spaced practice
- Review immediately before use
- Use multiple memory codes to improve retrieval.

In addition, be sure your children know the meanings of all abbreviations that are used in content areas. Have your children repeat to you what they heard and remembered of the directions. Reduce tension when your children forget, but be sure they perform tasks correctly.

During the test

Practice tests at home before the test. Have your children pretend that they are in the real test. Do this for no more than fifteen minutes. Remind them to do what they do at the practice test in the real test at school.

Teach your children to relax. Have them clear their minds of negative thoughts. Let them tell you what they are thinking. Teach them to concentrate totally on remembering the information they need to know.

When you give them a practice test, change the directions slightly. Have them ask you to write the directions for them. Have them practice asking questions until they remember the changes.

As soon as your children get the practice test, they should write down the material they know and then use it during the test. They can add to the material as they take the test.

They should quickly answer the questions they know. If there are questions they cannot answer, they should skip over those questions. They should put a marker beside any questions they skip. After they finish, they should return to missed questions from the back of the test to the front. If they still do not remember, they should again skip the questions and try a different problem until the answer to the skipped problem pops into their head. They can go immediately and write the answer.

As your children take the practice test, they should remember the memory aids they used and keep track of that information. They can write the clues or the information to help them answer their questions.

When your children finish the test and still have questions they cannot remember, they should do the relaxation exercises. While they are doing them, they need to tell themselves positive encouragement. They need to give themselves positive self-statements.

After they have answered all the questions, they should review the answers in the opposite directions from the first order that they took the test. If they started at the beginning, they should check by starting at the end. They should read the entire test again. They should mark questions they think are incorrect, but not change them. After they finish going through the check, they should return to the marked questions and read them again. They may see that they truly were incorrect or that they read them incorrectly while checking.

After the test

When your children receive the actual and practice tests back, they should go through them and determine why they made any errors. If they are able to bring the school test home, go through it with them. Have them tell you why they have the incorrect answer and how the correct answer is better. Make sure that they understand and correct each error.

After correcting the errors, your children should review all the errors and see if they are due to their processing. If they have earned below a B-, they should take the test again. While your children review, compliment them on the correct answers. Help them to tell themselves positive self-statements. As they review, they are learning how they operate under stress. Point out to them the strengths that they showed.

Whenever possible, contact parents of other students in your children's classes. Check if they will help your children study and learn how to perform better in classes. You can monitor the studying at your home.

Additional compensations

Check the results from the *GPI* to be sure that all compensations are taught to your children. You will see great improvements in their performance as they learn to adapt to their ability. Add additional compensations into the practice test session. Ask them which compensations they remembered while taking the actual test.

Information for the formal educational plan

Make sure that the compensations that were recorded in the *GPI* report are included in the educational plan for your children. These compensations should be enacted for both classroom tests and standardized tests.

Chapter 8

Spelling

Spelling becomes a difficult process because spelling requires writing (putting the word on paper or a computer), long-term memory (remembering the sounds and letters of the word), short-term memory (remembering the word and ideas wanted), vision (seeing what was written), and hearing (when the spelling test is dictated). Because all of these processes are essential for accurate spelling, spelling tests can be particularly stressful for your children. In this chapter, we discuss ways you can help them be successful in this process. We discuss:

- Connecting the sound of letters with the shape of the words.
- Singing words to hear the sounds better.
- Writing and spelling.
- Taking spelling tests
- Additional adjustments
- Compensations for the educational plan

Connecting the sound of letters with the shape of the words

When your children learn the spellings of words, be sure they are not just memorizing the order of the letters. Check that they understand that the letters are picked because of the sounds that they make. They should listen for the sounds of the word and match those sounds with the letters as they write.

Also, when learning spelling words, your children should connect the sound of the letters with the **shape** of the word. When they finish and have the correct spelling, point out the shape of the word. They can draw around the word to see that the words have shapes and letters and sounds. The shapes of the words can help them to remember how the words looked. They can use the shapes to help them check the spelling.

Singing words to hear the sounds better

If your children sing the words, they can hear the individual sounds better. Singing can slow down the listening process so that they can hear each sound better. As they write each letter, they need to hear the sound, see the letter, and feel their hand writing the word. When possible, they should sing words that are difficult for them while they are writing at home. Singing should slow down the sounds enough for them to hear the individual parts of the words. If they are in a place where they cannot sing the words, they can remember what the words sounded like when they did sing them.

When your children listen for the sounds of the words, they may hear that the vowels make many different sounds. This is because they may hear the different sounds formed as they go through the formation of a vowel. For example, the letter a sound makes the long *a* sound plus a long *e*, then a short *i*, and a short *u.* As your children listen to the word, they may hear all the changes the vowels make as they form the words. They will need help with these sounds so that they can hear them and identify which sound should be used in the spelling of the word. Be sure to help them hold onto the vowel sound that is needed for the word so that they can identify the correct sounds. They may need quite a bit of help to hold onto the correct vowel sound.

Writing and spelling

When your children are writing their assignments, they should put their thoughts on paper and not worry about spelling. After their thoughts are recorded, they can go back and correct spelling. Whenever possible, they should write directly onto a computer with a spell checker. They need to learn that the spell checker will not check for similar sounding words. It also may not be able to understand their misspellings.

Your children will need to learn how to ask for correct spellings whenever they are unsure. They will need help reading the words the spell checker offers and choosing the correct spellings. They may need help with spelling for the rest of their lives.

Taking spelling tests

In your children's compensations from the *General Processing Inventory (GPI),* you will find information for the teacher. The most important requirement for success on spelling tests is to have the teacher count the number of *letters* of the words rather than the number of words.

For example: The teacher can count the actual letters of the words tested and then grade on the percent of letters correctly used – even when they are out of order. For example, cta for cat is still correct *after* your children turn the letters around to cat. When teachers grade by letters, their assessments are actually more accurate than when they grade by word. This grading will demonstrate that your children are being quite successful at mastering the spelling process.

Additional adjustments

Check the results from the *GPI* to be sure that all the compensations that your children need to be successful are being used at school. These are all the requirements for vision, hearing, writing, long-term memory retrieval, and short-term memory retrieval. It is essential that all of these adjustments are included for success in spelling.

Compensations for the educational plan

All the compensations listed in the *GPI* should be included in your children's educational plan. Complete your part of the plan from the *GPI* in helping your children successfully get words correctly spelled. In homework that is not spelling, check that the teacher does not take off for spelling errors. The spelling errors should be marked, and your children should correct them, but their grade should not be affected by the errors. Your children should use a spell checker, peer tutor, you, or editing marks to make corrections. These adaptations should be included in the educational plan.

Chapter 9

Time Management and Life Adjustments

The problems caused by processing errors can be aggravated by many things. The weather, good events, bad events, and illness can affect your children's performance. In this chapter, we talk about what to do when the adjustments work and how to help your children adjust their behavior when adjustments do not work.

The errors identified by the *General Processing Inventory (GPI)* affect all areas of life. When your children learn to manage their social and personal life better, school life also improves and vice versa. In this chapter we discuss:

- Talking accurately
- Hearing correctly
- Having fun with your children's errors
- Living in peace with your children's friends, family, and others.
- Life is for living (remembering to adjust and forgetting to adjust}
- Bad/good weather adjustments (check your weather sense)
- Happy and sad days can be bad for processing!!
- Are your children feeling ill?

- Good news (your children are getting better each day!!)

Talking accurately

When your children misspeak, they are not aware that this is happening. They may become frustrated when other people do not respond to them as they would expect. You can help them to clarify by teaching them to ask, "What did you hear me say?"

If people did not hear what your children thought they said, they should learn to say, "I meant to say...." They should practice saying what they wanted to say rather than arguing about what they thought they said. Practice these behaviors with them when they become frustrated.

For example: One person ordered Mountain Dew at a restaurant. When it came, he was upset that he did not receive Dr. Pepper. Everyone at the table and the waitress heard him order incorrectly. He had learned to say, "I meant to order Dr. Pepper. Would you be able to change this drink?" He got the drink he wanted.

Hearing correctly

Your children's hearing will also create frustration. When they hear, they may hear differently from what was actually said. They need to learn to say, "I heard you say... What did you mean to say?" Again, they will need to learn how to avoid arguing about what they actually heard compared with what was intended. Their hearing processing errors will alter what they hear others say.

Practice having your children question what is heard and practice asking for people to repeat what they say. Teach them how to adjust their response from being frustrated to asking for the information again.

Having fun with your children's errors

Your children may already have learned how to be silly when they mishear or misspeak. You can help them to use laughter when misunderstandings happen. Help them to laugh at the confusion that can occur, but to correct the errors so that they communicate well with others.

Help your children learn to relax about the miscommunication. Help them to learn to ask for clarification about communication so that they are communicating more accurately and enjoying the relationships of those around them.

You will hear the argument start with, "You just said..." This is followed by a denial, like, "No, I didn't," and the battle is on. You may be able to help your children avoid this type of argument by asking for clarification of meaning rather than disputing over specific words.

Help them to stop and say, "I heard you say..." This may take a lifetime to learn! Arguments will gradually become fewer as they learn to ask for meaning rather than arguing about the words.

Mishearing is frustrating! When your children mishear you, respond with, "I meant to say..." Modeling the correct behavior will help them learn to use the expressions.

Living in peace with your children's friends, family, and others

Remind your children that they do not hear accurately nor speak accurately. When they start to argue about what was said or not said, help them to take a moment to breathe and then ask what was meant and state what they meant. They will need time to practice living without arguing about words.

Life is for living (remembering to adjust and forgetting to adjust)

While you are adjusting to your children's problems, be sure to take time away from them and your intense training. Spend time with other adults doing things unrelated to your children. Keeping your equilibrium is critical for being able to stay calm enough for your children.

In addition, take time to do things with your other children. Spend your time wisely and let them know that you appreciate their help with the process. Teach your other children how to help your children with processing problems so that they can be part of the progress and solution.

Finally, do things with your children that are not related to school. Spend time doing parenting that is not related to their adaptations and school. Appreciate them for themselves and treat them normally as much as possible.

Bad/good weather adjustments (check your weather sense)

The difference in air pressure systems can affect processing. Watch out for storms and changes in weather. Alert your children to watching for subtle changes when the weather changes. Help them to watch out for misprocessing when they see changes in the weather. They need to be especially careful at school when the weather changes.

Bright, sunny days after days of rain or snow can have the same effect as storms coming in after great weather. Changes in temperature can create processing problems. Check the weather with your children to help them learn to be ready for checking their own input and output.

Happy and sad days can be bad for processing!

When emotionally charged situations happen, the emotions can affect processing. Emotions occur with happy situations as well as sad ones. Special occasions can affect your children. Help them remember to take an extra moment when emotional situations happen at home or at school.

Some special occasions can be holidays, visits from special people, vacation days, and snow days. These can be exciting for your children. They may not be able to control the excitement and their processing at the same time. Even small children who do not have processing problems have difficulty expressing their good and negative emotions. You can calm your children by helping them realize that emotions can be controlled by breathing slowly and just talking about their feelings. They can practice breathing slowly and saying that they are very happy and excited and feel the emotions subside.

Are your children feeling ill?

At times, your children may have a cold or the flu. You may find that processing goes awry when your children are ill. You can help them adjust as they fight off a cold or the flu. Wait to do make up work for school until they can process accurately again.

Good news (Your children are getting better each day!)

The best part of this process is when you start seeing progress. Expect that every day, your children will be a little bit better at processing material. Each week, you will see that they have grown. Every month, school work will be easier than the month before. As your children grow into using the compensations, they will still be working very hard. The difference will be that their hard work will pay off in successful performance at school, better relations at home, and positive self-image development as they improve each day.

Chapter 10

The *General Processing Inventory (GPI)*

In this chapter, we review the six error categories of processing problems. Throughout the book, I have referred to the *General Processing Inventory (GPI)*[17] as the tool for identifying the errors and then giving you the path to follow for your children. In this chapter, we look at what the *GPI* does and how you can use its results. We review the compensations to get around those errors that are identified through the *GPI*. We discuss the following:

- Identification of processing problems
- Review of adaptations - compensations
- Final review of six error categories
- How to proceed

Identification of processing problems

There are millions of different ways that people can misprocess information. Your children have to process the written and spoken word and respond with speaking and writing. In addition, your children have to remember the thread of the conversation and information just given. Also, your children need to remember the

---

[17] See Appendix B.

past events that may be brought into the conversation.

Just to write a sentence, your children have to remember how to spell each word, how to form the letters of those words, which words they wanted to use, what their reason for writing was, and which details to omit. Knowing that they are operating irregularly is critical so that they can learn to communicate accurately. Once they know what is malfunctioning, they can learn to adjust for the errors that are identified.

These processing problems can be condensed into the six categories of

- Visual input
- Hearing input
- Writing output
- Speaking output
- Retrieval from short-term memory storage
- Retrieval from long-term memory storage

The errors are similar in the different categories. Garbling of information consists of

- Reversing symbols, (37 for 73 or tac for cat)
- Substituting symbols and words, (+ for x or ? for !)
- Repeating words and symbols, (555 for 55 or This is is an example for This is an example.)

- Dropping words and symbols, (21 for 221 or th for the)
- Adding words and symbols, (732 for 72 or threre for three)
- Agnosias, which are inability to see and read certain symbols; for example, **coin agnosia** means inability to recognize the different coins and their values.
- Dyscopia, the inability to copy, involves both reading and writing. Your children will not be able to copy accurately.
- Many additional errors are identified through the *GPI*.

Review of adaptations (compensations)

When your children are diagnosed with learning disabilities, the diagnosis may have included some hints of what was causing the problems in school. These disruptions are very serious and cause your children to be unable to communicate accurately. These problems will not go away, but your children can learn to get around them and to compensate for them. The results of the *GPI* list the specific compensations your children will need to learn to be successful both in school and in life.

In the rest of this chapter, I will tell about some of the symptoms that are covered in the *GPI* that I developed to help uncover specific processing errors. The *GPI* results include compensations for your children's specific errors. Compensations tell you, your children, your children's teachers, and your children's peers what to do to get around the problems that are identified through the *GPI*. You have probably recognized problems that your children have in the descriptions presented in the previous chapters. Not all disruptions and compensations are described in this book, so be sure to have your children take the *GPI* so that their specific and complete problems can be clearly identified. In addition, you will need to learn all the compensations that are listed for them in the results of your children's *GPI* report.

Finding the specific processing problems that affect your children is the first step in correcting for them. There are many errors that can occur in each of the six error categories, making the possibilities of error over several million. These different errors affect processing in different ways. Your children will not be experiencing every one of these many errors, so knowing which errors are occurring is critical.

Knowing how to compensate for your children's specific errors is the important second step included in the *GPI*. This chapter includes a general description of the compensations, too. I have included examples of errors that could be identified through the *GPI*. A complete evaluation includes testing for many more errors. The errors rarely occur alone, making the identification more difficult. The *GPI* is designed to help find and correct for the following errors:

Visual input

The input from your children's eyes may not be accurate. Things garble and move and shift. For example, one student could not find a shelf in a closet because it kept moving! Other students reported that the letters on the page would change each time they looked at the words. Some saw the top of the page as white and the bottom of the page as black. Others saw squiggly lines coming out of letters. Still other students saw the middle of the letters as black spots. Also, students reported that the page of print was wavy.

What do your children see when they look at a page of print? Ask them to describe what happens. Write down what they say and give these descriptions to their professional helpers and medical doctors. These are clues about the physical nature of their problems.

When disruption of vision is occurring, the letters, words, and symbols are not stable. For example, when your children's eyes operate normally, they are flipping the image from the retina to their brain. At times with visual distortion, this flip may not occur, so letters appear upside down. A *p* would look like a *b*, or a *d* would become a *q*.

At other times, your children's brain may twist images. Then the letters in a word would become mixed up. Instead of seeing the letters for **Ohio**, they could see **Ooih** If the two problems just described happened at the same time, they would see *qgo* for *dog* or *6* for *9.*

Letters and words could flip sideways. Now your children see a *b* for *d* reversal. A word like *saw* becomes *was*. Now scrambling gets quite involved. Instead of seeing words on a page, your children see letter combinations that make no sense.

One adult reported that she had her brothers and sisters read the stories to her so that she could memorize them. She told how as a child she had wondered how anyone knew that all those spellings for horse meant the same word. She "figured out" that reading must be memorizing the stories and telling them back. Fortunately, a great reading teacher helped her learn to decipher the written page better!

What happens when the eye does not track across the letters correctly? Your children may repeat letters, drop words, add symbols, and skip lines of print. Now you can understand better that your children have to be brilliant to be able to read at all with these types of distortions happening. The first thing you can do immediately is to read every word with your children. I wrote about what to do to improve reading in Chapters 2 and 3. There are many ways you can help your children overcome these incredible distortions (There are many more distortions, too!)

The *GPI* lists the specific errors with the letters, symbols, and words your children confused. Previous chapters have compensations for you and your children as they relate to specific tasks in school.

Hearing input

Hearing (auditory processing) errors are a problem for many people because the hearing garbling problems are rarely checked. Auditory problems also are the only problems that occur by themselves. Your children may be hearing inaccurately and acting out because of their inaccurate hearing. When they learn to compensate, they will become calmer and more receptive to speaking and communication.

The auditory input problems interact with the speech output problems. See below in speech output for additional information.

Speaking output

Hearing input and speaking output processing issues create problems in families, as well as at school. In fact, here is a story about a family that was going to therapy for years. The mother and the daughter both could not hear accurately and did not speak accurately. Neither was aware of this fact. They fought constantly. Their constant fighting was the reason they were in therapy. When, through the *GPI,* the mother learned that the daughter had the hearing **and** speech issues, she recognized that she had similar behaviors. Both learned to say, "I thought I heard you say... What did you mean to say?" They also learned to say, "I meant to say..." Within a few months, they were out of therapy.

If your children do not hear what others say and do not say what they mean to say, they are trapped in a confusing world. They think that people are saying awful things to them. They do not understand why others respond so negatively to their kind statements.

In fact, they may be hearing incorrectly and speaking incorrectly at the same time. They will be angry and frustrated almost all the time. When they learn to ask about meanings rather than argue about words that cannot be reviewed, they will open the doors to successful communication.

In speech, your children may have all of the symptoms of reversals, dropping words, repeating words, saying the wrong words, adding words, and many other problems. These errors will be confusing to people around them. In addition, your children are hearing what others say with errors of dropping words, substituting words, hearing repeated words, not understanding the garbling, and many other errors.

The *GPI* has a list of the errors your children speak and hear. There will be many compensations for you to try. In Chapter 9, we discussed how to adapt to these errors at home.

Writing output

According to my research, the most common area of disruption in processing was writing. Your children will not be aware that they are making errors. They believe they are writing correctly. Later, they may be able to see the errors and be stunned. They need to know that the errors are not indicating their lack of intelligence, but are evidence of their physical problems.

I will describe these errors briefly here because, in the writing chapter, I have already showed you different types of writing errors and given examples of how they appear. Your children's specific errors may occur with definite letters, symbols, words, or combinations of symbols. Use the compensations from the writing chapter to help your children through the educational activities that are required of them in school.

Capitalization *F* and *t*, *M* and *n*

Since *f* and *t* are frequently written incorrectly, many children always use capital *F* and lower case *t* to separate them. This is problematic because capitalization rules are ignored through this process. *M* and *n* are frequently separated in the same way. Do your children capitalize certain letters most of the time? What is a similar letter that is being separated for them through this process?

Dropping letters or strokes

As your children write a *w*, they drop half of it and write only *v*. A similar error is writing *n* for *m*. When they write words, they may drop endings, such as *-tion*, *-s*, *-ed*, and *-ble*. Sometimes the middle of the word is missing like *chiren* for *children.*

Adding and repeating letters or symbols

When your children write, they may add additional letters, symbols, or words. Now their hands continue to write after they have stopped commanding it to write. For example, they *write*

write a word twice. They could also add letters as in the word ***little*** written as ***littttle***. They do not see the extra words and letters when they read over the work.

Perseveration is failure to move on to the next symbol or thought. Sections of a word may be repeated or a single symbol may be repeated. For example, ***16*** becomes ***116.*** Another way your children can perseverate is to use a letter word or symbol from what someone else said or wrote. For example, the teacher could ask, ***"What is 3 + 4?"*** Your children could answer, ***4***, instead of ***7***. Another way to perseverate is to give a previous answer instead of the intended answer. For example, the previous answer may have been choice ***a.*** The next answer should be ***b***; but your children write ***a***, instead.

In the previous chapters, I told you how to help your children avoid and get around these errors in regular classroom settings. Teachers, peers, and you can assist them throughout this process.

The results of the *GPI* have the lists of the letters, symbols, and typical errors your children make. The compensations for these errors are also included. In chapters 2 through 9 are the practical suggestions for adaptations as they relate to specific areas in school and at home.

Retrieval from short-term memory storage

Once your children go to school, society has certain expectations about what they are able to do. We assume that they can remember what we have just told them to do. For example, when we say that they should sit down, we expect them to sit. Your children may not have that ability. The *GPI* checks if your children can remember what they have just heard or read. Your children may have difficulty remembering what they just read or heard. They try to remember it by saying it over and over again to themselves. Then suddenly, they can no longer say it. The information is gone.

Also, they may remember information slightly differently from what they heard. You may say to them to go to the kitchen. They will go to their bedroom instead. In school, the directions may be to circle answers, but they underline them. They may be told to do the even problems, but they do the odd ones.

Their inability to remember what was just said or written makes following directions very difficult. They seem like they are being deliberately naughty, when in fact, they do not remember what to do.

Their frustration with getting in trouble for not remembering makes them forget even faster. Soon they stop trying to remember and may become discipline problems. They do not try to follow the rules because they cannot figure them out or remember them. They do whatever attracts their attention and do not worry about the consequences because they are usually in trouble anyway.

Learning that they cannot remember the directions is critical to your children's emotional welfare. They need to learn how to keep track of directions and to have ways to record them so they can replay them when they drop from their memory. Your communication with them will greatly improve as you remember: They cannot remember what you just told them to do! They may not be acting disobediently; they may be forgetting.

Helping your children to organize information so that they can use it will help them tremendously at home, school, and with their friends. Their behavior will improve dramatically as they learn to cope with remembering and following directions.

Check the *GPI* results for the specific suggestions for your children. Also, in Chapters 2 through 9 are some compensations for particular activities. These compensations will help you and your children with specific homework assignments. In addition, your children can use the compensations at home as well as at school.

Retrieval from long-term memory storage

Many facts are stored in your children's long-term memory. They have links to these facts so that they can access and use them. Sometimes your children's links do not work accurately. Here is an example of how that disruption can occur:

Your children may spend hours trying to remember only ten spelling words for a first grade spelling test. When they take the test, they get all ten words wrong. They may drop, substitute, repeat, and flip letters. In addition to these errors, they may forget the order of the letters. We can show their teachers how to grade by counting the number of letters in all the words and score them for the number of letters they get correct.

In their regular studying, your children have to learn to organize the material so that they can recall it. Sometimes watching a television show can help trigger their memory. Sometimes studying in many different places around the house may help them code the information. They have to review and review and review. They should review at school until they are told to put away their notes.

Your children can graduate from high school and college with honors, but memory retrieval will make that accomplishment a more difficult task. Their ability to focus and to stick with a task will help them do well. They must never give up, but instead they will need to continually study.

One area that is extremely important in their development will be learning and using the 400 basic addition, subtraction, multiplication, and division facts. For example, they need to know 3*3 = 9 and the other 399 basic facts. I worked together with students as they told me what they saw in the numbers. I developed a way to see the answers from the problems themselves and wrote a series of eight booklets which use this method to remember the 400 basic math facts.[18] You can use the eight booklets to help your children remember the facts and help you to organize other material they need to learn.

Final review of the six error categories

Here is a brief description of all six error groups of processing errors. Remember to use the results from the *GPI* to find out your children's specific errors. Then apply the compensations so that your children can be successful.

Visual input

A single three-letter word can appear in over a thousand different ways, depending on the

---

[18] The eight booklets are available from the author. See Appendix B.

error that occurs. All the letters could reverse, flip upside down, and go sideways. The possibilities increase as each error is introduced.

All these errors happen in an irregular manner. In addition, the center of the letters can be absent; there can be trailing threads from each corner of the letters; the letters can all combine into a black mass; the letters can swirl, pop, move in waves, and distort in other ways. Your children may be learning to read with all these errors and are extremely talented. They may not realize how much distortion is occurring. They will assume everyone sees as they do. Once they learn their specific distortions, they can readily adapt.

Hearing input
Any of the errors of vision occur in hearing, too. Words are heard backwards; words substitute for each other; and the noise of a room interferes with the sounds of speech. Your children cannot ignore all the sounds of the room. Ask them if the sounds interfere this way:

- Do you hear the sound of your clothes on the desk as you try to write?
- Does the sound of all the pencils scratching on the paper hurt your ears?
- Are the lights a noisy sound in the room?

- When the fan goes on for the heating or air conditioning, does it stop your thinking?
- Are your own breathing sounds distracting?

Ask if any other sounds have been distracting them. They cannot drown out all the noises because they hear more than you do. When their hearing is tested, they may actually hear much more than others do. The extra sound input is extremely distracting.

Speaking output

Even though your children may want to say, "I like that sweater," the words that they actually say are, "That sweater is goofy." They may be very embarrassed by these speech problems. They say the wrong words, use the wrong tone, confuse themselves and their friends, and are quite unaware what is happening. The garbling of their speech creates major problems in all areas of their lives. They may learn to cover up their errors by pretending they are joking. Other people may become annoyed with their "inappropriate" jokes, which are actually garbling of their speech that they cannot control.

Writing output, Retrieval from short-term memory storage, and Retrieval from long-term memory storage

Similar errors occur in in the writing output and retrieval from the memory systems. The words, letters, and symbols become garbled and unrecognizable. Spell checkers do not know what was written. Your children cannot find the information they have carefully stored. They cannot repeat what was just said to them. Obviously these errors are critical. They mask true ability. Once your children learn how to overcome the errors, they will be highly successful. We have called these errors processing errors. As we saw earlier, the errors are caused by physical problems and have nothing to do with your children's intelligence.

How to proceed

Once the specific errors are clearly identified, the compensations can begin. We will talk about the next steps in the final chapter. The steps are related to your children's work in school and at home.

Chapter 11

Next Steps

The previous chapters introduced you to the Geiman Method for helping your children overcome processing problems. The identification of symptoms, training to overcome identified problems, and completion of the program for adapting to your children's processing errors was briefly described. In this chapter, we will review what you need to do now to activate the program for your children by using these steps:

- Identifying the specific problems
- Treating the problems as physical instead of cognitive
- Rapidly reviewing all content and skills for learning
- Applying the compensations while reviewing
- Finding resources and resource people.
- Living life

Identifying the specific problems
Now that you have an idea about the root causes of the problems your children have been experiencing, it is time to find out exactly what their specific issues are. In order to apply the

correct compensations, you must know which specific problems are affecting their performance. The tool I recommend using is the *General Processing Inventory (GPI).*[19] The *GPI* is written specifically to identify the problems your children have in classroom settings as well as during the rest of their lives. In addition, the results are given in terms to be used by them specifically. Also, recommendations are given for you their parents, for their peers, and also for their teachers. These recommendations will help you know what you can do to help your children to be successful in school and at home.

Treating the problems as physical instead of cognitive

Once you have the identification of the areas that need compensations, start using the compensations from the *GPI* as you communicate with your children. Use just one or two compensations at a time until you get used to using all of them. Let your children be involved with picking the compensations to use.

Your children have exhibited brilliance by being able to operate as long as they have without the compensations that they need. Now your focus can be on the physical compensations that are essential for your children. When their

---

[19] Available from the author. See Appendix B.

problems are identified as physical through the *GPI*, professionals will readily use the compensations that address the physical nature of their issues. Your children's problems of learning are not cognitive. They have clearly demonstrated their cognitive ability by working without the compensations for their physical problems.

Since your children's problems are physical, they will grow stronger and more adept as they begin to use the compensations. They will gradually take over the care of their education as they master the use of the compensations. At first, while they are learning how to use compensations, they will have to focus on using them. As they become comfortable with the compensations, the adaptations will fall into the background. Then they will be able to use the compensations to learn material for school.

Just as children who suddenly lose their vision would need additional assistance at first, your children will need more assistance at the beginning of their training. Your goal is to remove yourself from your children's studying as soon as they are able to study on their own. Just as children with broken legs need to use crutches until they are able to start using their legs, so your children will need your assistance until they are able to learn on their own. For most children, this may be six to eighteen months. Your children's teachers will be able to help you determine when your children are ready to do things on their own.

During the training process, you may notice that your children will want to become independent. When this happens, let them do things on their own and stay available to them for when they may need help. As they learn harder material and grow through the educational program, they may need assistance off and on. Be aware that their performance will improve, but their symptoms will remain.

On the other hand, your children may need to be encouraged to try studying on their own. If your children are reluctant to try compensations on their own, you may need to create distance between you and them as they study. While they study, be in the next room. When they ask you for help, tell them you will be right there as soon as you... (Have a task to complete) and then complete a task before you help them. Gradually, they will learn that they can work on their own.

Rapidly reviewing all content and skills for learning
Science, social studies, grammar, and health
Volunteer to help with the review of past educational material. When your children

review, use text books from previous grade levels. To review, use the chapter questions at the ends of each chapter. When your children can answer all the questions, go on to the next chapter. If they are interested in a topic, go through that topic and then go to the next chapter.

When your children cannot answer a question, use the index and the table of contents to show them how to locate the answer quickly. Be sure that they understand the meaning of the question and the answer. Continue with the end of the chapter questions. Review chapter material in depth whenever they miss a question.

When you review the material for kindergarten through second grade, you will complete an entire grade review in about one to two days. You are just using the questions at the end of each chapter. After you review a chapter in one subject, do a chapter in another subject. Keep changing subjects until you have reviewed all the chapters for each grade level.

Do the same for first and second grades. When you have reviewed all of a book, start with another book on the same subject at the next grade level. If your children are above second grade, they should be able to review all of kindergarten, first, and second grade in one to two weeks (one or more days per grade). Third grade reviews and above will take more time.

Math review

Review math in this same way. In addition, be sure to have your children practice problems until they can do them quickly and correctly. Use the Geiman math fact books to review the basic 400 math facts.[20] Younger children will just need to review the addition and subtraction facts. With older children, start reviewing the multiplication and division facts first. After these are learned, if your children wish, you can go through the addition and subtraction memorization by patterns using the Geiman booklets.

Reading review

If your children have difficulty reading, have them review the reading process in a different way from the chapter reviews described above. Read all of the stories and review the phonics lessons. Read the complete stories with them as discussed in the reading chapter. At first, they only need to read a word or sentence per page. You read the rest as fluently and quickly as possible. Later, have them read a paragraph per page. Finally, switch back and forth by pages.

---

[20] Available from the author. See Appendix B

Eventually, they will read multiple pages and ask you to read short sections.

As you review the rest of the material for higher grades, you will slow down to adjust to the extra content of the material. Keep reviewing a chapter in each subject area by using the questions at the end of the chapters. Go deeper when they need more information. Go quickly when they already know the material. The purpose of the review is to help your children see that they know all the material and that they can learn quickly and accurately. Also, you will be applying the compensations so that they become used to them.

Applying the compensations while reviewing

There are several reasons to review all previous school material.

- Reviewing shows your children that they can do a lot of work quickly.
- Reviewing lets your children know that they have learned all the material they needed to learn.
- Reviewing gives you an opportunity to show them how to use the compensations while doing actual school work.

While your children are reviewing, practice new compensations each day of review.

Introduce at least two to three new compensations each day and maintain the compensations from the previous days. In this way, your children can see that they really do understand what they are learning. They will see that their misprocessing does interfere with their ability to read, write, speak, hear, and retrieve material accurately. They will begin to see their specific errors as problems similar to needing glasses.

As they are reviewing, they are learning how to manage their studying and learning. Introducing the compensations each day is a very important component of the review. Make sure that you completely introduce all the compensations given in the *GPI* report.

Finding resources and resource people

Throughout this book, I have given you many ideas about how to help your children. At times, you may feel quite alone and very frustrated. These are valid feelings, but the fact is that many people are interested in your children's success.

These people are ready to support and encourage you along your path. They have resources and ideas to help you, too. Your children's teachers, principals, special education teachers, special education supervisors, guidance counselors, and superintendent have a special interest in your children's success. Many of these people will be able to help you find specific resources that are available in your district.

When people are helpful, be sure to thank them and to ask how you can help them, too. In addition, if people do not know the answers to your problems, realize that you are a pioneer in helping children with processing issues. Keep an open door and wait for change. Sometimes a few years can make a huge difference in a person's attitude.

For example, one teacher was quite upset that my son was placed into her gifted class. He had to be moved to a different class at the request of the principal and superintendent. Five years later, this same teacher was my daughter's teacher for gifted classes. My daughter had many more problems than my son. The teacher was delighted to help her because she had seen the success of my son. She remembered enjoying knowing and working with my son! We allowed her to keep remembering the situation that way.

Your children's success will answer a lot of questions that people have about what you are doing. You may need to wait to let their success be obvious. Another story: a different teacher asked my son, in seventh grade, what would happen if he got a D or an F on his report card. He replied that he would not have to worry about anything because I would kill him. The teacher reported me to the superintendent as being an abuser.

Fortunately, the superintendent had already visited our home and watched what I was doing. In addition, we had had many conversations about how to use what I was learning to help other students in his district. These conversations were initiated by me at first and then later by him. I did not find out about the accusations until years later. The superintendent had already known what I was doing and how I cared for my children without abusing them. He knew that my son was exaggerating and not relating facts. A professional, positive relationship with the people at school prevented a huge problem!

Develop a reputation for helping the district and being a calm, credible parent. Help your children by maintaining a positive relationship with your district's personnel. They give you the materials for your children's learning. In addition, you may have opportunities to assist them in school and out of school. You may also be involved in helping to educate the educators about helping children with processing problems.

What else do you do? Please feel free to contact me to add your adaptations to the ever-growing list of ways to help children with processing problems!

Living life

Your most important role in this entire process is to maintain a life that is pleasant and as normal as possible. As soon as possible when your children come home from school, have them complete their homework and then be free for the rest of the evening. Expect age appropriate behavior. Explain that frustration is acceptable, but expressing it in positive ways must be taught.

As much as possible, maintain a family that is supportive and kind. Teach principles of life as your children grow. Be sure your children focus on living. Helping your children to develop a positive attitude toward your family and people they contact outside of your home is your most important role.

For example, I overheard my son explain his auditory problems to a friend, "I hear a lot more than most people. This means that I can get confused. I will have to ask you to repeat sometimes. Is that okay?"

The two shook hands and never talked about the problems again. They were in fourth grade. They stayed friends throughout school.

Enjoy the journey as much as possible. Feel free to contact me with comments, questions, and successes.

I wish you well as you go forward and help your children to be successful!

Appendix A

What the Author Believes about Being a Christian

At times in this book, I have referred to God and His direction in my building the Geiman Method to help children and adults with processing problems. I am not a special person; God is a special spiritual being. He will do for you what He did for me and many other people in the world. You do not need to be a Christian to enact the procedures of the book. The following is an explanation of my beliefs in regard to who God is, and that He cares about every single human being deeply and kindly.

I believe that God cares about you and your children's problems. He did not create the problems, evil did. There was a spiritual war between God and all evil. God already won when He conquered all evil and death. We can be a part of His victorious family by asking Him to live in and through us in our lives.

If you are interested in having God direct your life and guide you in caring for your children, He will be happy to do that. God is a spirit and is present whether you invite Him to guide you or do not. He is the source of all good things. Evil is real and is controlled by spiritual beings who rebelled against God. We will honor and serve either God and His ways or evil and its ways.

To serve God is a way we can choose to live. God is wiser than the wisest person or group of people because He made us all. God will direct us about what to do in very gentle, kind ways. He will never force us to do anything against our will. He only desires good for you and your children.

To become a member of God's family, we need to be adopted into God's family by asking Him to save us from all evil and forgive us for any evil we have done. Just ask God to love and care for you, and He will. I know this because He came as a real person named Jesus to live a perfect life for you and me and to pay the price for anything wrong we have done. He came 2000 years ago and lived and died, but then rose from the dead to prove He was conqueror over death and evil and truly God.

I cannot tell you about all the good things God has done or will do. Many things are written about Him. The most accurate writings are in the Bible. I suggest that you start in the middle of the book with the New Testament part and read Mark. Then read Revelation to find out about where we are going.

Wherever you live in the world, you will be able to watch special Christian television networks that will tell you about God in more detail. Trinity Broadcasting Network (TBN), Daystar, and Word are some of the twenty-four hour Christian information networks. In addition, most areas have Christian radio stations to encourage and educate you. You then can find people who also are living in God's family if you contact any of the presenters on these networks or radio stations. You can be a member of God's family because Jesus is the God and man who paid for your entry into His Father's family.

Here is what I believe it means to become a Christian:

God is perfect and holy. If we have done or thought anything impure, we are not holy. That means that if we met God in person, God's holiness would consume us. Therefore, God decided to punish someone else for our sins (wrong things we have thought or done). The person God punished in place of us is Jesus. Jesus offered himself freely for our punishment. We can accept His payment for our sins. That makes us Christians.

When Jesus died, he freely gave himself to pay for our sins. No one killed him; he chose to die for everyone. When he died, he paid for all the sins of everyone who ever lived before him, lived when he lived, or lived after him. That includes me, you, and your family.

To accept this wonderful gift of freedom from all we have ever done wrong or will do wrong until we die, we

1. Admit that we have done wrong
2. Ask God to forgive us because Jesus paid for all the wrong we have done
3. Thank God for forgiving us

Once we have asked God to forgive us, we can now ask Him to live in us. He will be constantly with us. We may or may not notice His guidance. We can ask Him to help us in every situation of life. He will be with us forever.

After we have become Christians, we next find a church that is a Christian church and join others to help us find out what God wants us to do with the rest of our lives. We are forgiven for all we ever did wrong. We are Christians.

Being a Christian means we are forgiven and can approach our holy God who loves us dearly.

All the world can be a Christian. All have been saved forever. I wish this for you and the entire world! If you want to contact me about your decision to be a member of God's family, you may email me: ruthgeiman@yahoo.com. Welcome into God's family.

Appendix B

Purchasing Materials and Tests

How to purchase the eight booklets, testing by the author, and training for purchase and administration of the *General Processing Inventory (GPI)*

Eight booklets

To buy copies of the eight booklets on addition/subtraction and multiplication/division facts, contact the author at ruthgeiman@yahoo.com.

Each booklet costs $10 pre-release and $15 after release. There are five multiplication/division booklets and four addition/subtraction books.

Testing by the author

To have your children or yourself tested by the author, you must make an appointment and travel to Columbus, Ohio. Testing is by appointment only. Cost is $750 per person for the three-hour evaluation and one-hour results session. Contact ruthgeiman@yahoo.com for details and appointments.

Training for purchase and administration of the *General Processing Inventory (GPI)*

If you wish to purchase the *GPI*, you must have a valid license as a psychologist, school psychologist, or teacher. In addition, you must be trained and licensed to administer the *GPI*. You receive a copy of the *GPI* only through training and licensure.

Training costs $3500 and includes the copy of the *GPI*, two manuals, test materials, answer sheets, and four evaluations of people of your choice as you are trained to administer, score, and write reports based on the *GPI*.

Contact ruthgeiman@yahoo.com for details and training opportunities.

Appendix C

Review of the of the Entire Book

Here is a brief review of all of the chapters of the entire book - overcoming the six processing errors identified through the *GPI*. Try the specific adjustments for each error to see if they work for your children. If they do, feel free to continue to use them. Be sure to involve others as you work through the processing errors. Check out the last section in each of chapters 3 through 8 for specific suggestions that should be included in your children's education plan.

You can use these chapters in different ways. You can read them straight through to see what material applies to your children. Another way to approach the book is to first read the chapters that seem to apply to your children. Then you can read the chapters that you skipped. You can also read the chapters that apply to the biggest issues that face your children at the present time and then return to the other chapters. The review of the rest of the book is to help you decide how to approach the information. In the book, we discussed the following topics:

Chapter 1: The Geiman Method

In this chapter, I introduced you to the Geiman Method which has demonstrated success in helping people overcome learning disabilities. Here I answered your questions by discussing the following topics:

- Your children's disability is real (the name does not matter)
- Your children's problems are probably physical
- Your children may be extremely impaired (comparison to Helen Keller)
- Processing problems are altered perceptions (an example)
- What you can expect
- What the Geiman Method is
- Why rapid success is possible
- How the Geiman Method can be enacted
- What should already be completed

Chapter 2: Reading Adjustments for Visual Distortion

Reading is one of the fundamental ways to gain knowledge. Any visual distortion can make reading intensely difficult. Reading skill is essential for early years of education and increases in importance at higher levels of education. For example, courses in both secondary and post-secondary education require a lot of outside reading. As a result, adapting for the visual distortion is critical.

We discussed the following:

- Visual distortion defined
- Alternate methods of reading information
- Essential compensation skills
- Checklist for specific reading errors
- Next steps
- Information for the instructional planning meeting

Chapter 3: Additional Reading Problems and Solutions

In this chapter, we identified common reading issues not related to the visual distortion. These problems can aggravate the visual distortion and need to be treated along with the distortion. We discussed:

- Analysis of why people do not read
- Difficulties embedded in the reading process
- Other issues
- Conclusions for the educational plan

Chapter 4: Suggestions for Writing Accurately

In my research, writing disruption was the processing problem that I most frequently observed. When your children write, they may not write as they intend and are quite unaware that they are miswriting. When they get an assignment back, they can be extremely frustrated by their errors. This chapter gave you the adaptations and compensations for writing so that you can help them demonstrate their ability through writing. We discussed:

- The physical nature of writing problems
- Alternate methods of recording information
- The second phase of writing
- Checking for specific writing errors
- Using the method: a case study
- What to do at the Instructional Planning meeting

Chapter 5: Studying and Homework

When your children have serious problems completing a task, they will avoid the task. In this chapter, we discussed how you can retrain your children so that they complete tasks when they are fresh enough to do them well. Creating schedules for doing unpleasant tasks helps your children learn to do them and do them well.

We covered:
- Worst tasks first
- Rewards for completing tasks
- Scheduling the unpleasant
- Completing all tasks as directed
- Passing through the four stages of learning when studying
- Identifying the stage necessary for a task and the level of study of the task
- Adaptations to be sure information is accurately recorded
- Sorting information to learn it
- Additional adaptations for studying (*GPI*)
- Entering information into the educational plan

Chapter 6: Math

There are only four operations in basic arithmetic: addition, subtraction, multiplication, and division. There are only a few types of real numbers, including counting, whole, integers, fraction forms, and irrationals. However, the combinations of these numbers can be overwhelming to your children. You can help them see the patterns in the numbers that will make math easier. Looking for patterns can help them learn to enjoy math. In this chapter, we discussed:

- Physical processing problems and how they affect learning math
- Recycling concepts for meaning
- Applying concepts to real life
- Asking questions for meaning
- Completing assignments (homework four steps)
- Using an assignment notebook
- Additional math ideas
- Information for the educational plan

Chapter 7: Taking Tests

Taking tests is actually an activity that takes place at school, but you can prepare your children so that taking tests becomes easier. Refer to their compensations from the *GPI*. We covered:

- Physical processing issues
- Test taking adaptations
- Additional compensations
- Information for the formal educational process

Chapter 8: Spelling

Spelling is sometimes a difficult process. Spelling tests can be particularly stressful for your children. In this chapter, we discussed ways you can help them in this process. We discussed:

- Connecting the sound of letters with the shape of the words
- Singing words to hear the sounds better
- Writing and spelling
- Taking spelling tests
- Additional adjustments
- Compensations for the educational plan

Chapter 9: Time Management and Life Adjustments

The problems caused by processing errors can be affected by many things. The weather, good events, bad events, and illness can affect your children's performance. In this chapter, we talked about what to do when the adjustments work and how to help your children adjust their behavior when adjustments do not work.

The errors identified by the *GPI* affect all areas of life. When your children learn to manage their social and personal life better, school life also improves and vice versa. In this chapter, we discussed:

- Talking accurately
- Hearing correctly
- Having fun with your children's errors
- Living in peace with your children's friends, family, and others
- Life is for living (remembering to adjust and forgetting to adjust)

- Bad/good weather adjustments (check your weather sense)
- Happy and sad days can be bad for processing!!
- Are your children feeling ill?
- Good news (your children are getting better each day!!)

Chapter 10: The *General Processing Inventory (GPI)*

In this chapter, we reviewed the six error categories of processing problems. Throughout the book, I referred to the *GPI* as the tool for identifying the errors and then gave you the path to follow for your children. In this chapter, we looked at what the *GPI* does and how you can use its results. We reviewed the *GPI* compensations to get around those errors that are identified through the *GPI*. We discussed the following:

- Identification of processing problems
- Review of adaptations (compensations)
- Final review of six error categories
- How to proceed

Chapter 11: Next Steps

The previous chapters introduced you to the Geiman Method for helping your children overcome processing problems. The identification of symptoms, training to overcome identified problems, and completion of the program for adapting to your children's processing errors were briefly described. In this chapter, we reviewed what you need to do now to activate the program for your children by using these steps:

- Identifying the specific problems
- Treating the problems as physical instead of cognitive
- Rapidly reviewing all content and skills for learning
- Applying the compensations while reviewing
- Living life

Appendix A: What the Author Believes about Being a Christian

Appendix B: Purchasing Materials and Tests

Appendix C: Review of the Entire Book

Appendix D: *General Processing Inventory (GPI)* Screening – Directions and Screening

Appendix D: GPI Screening

Directions for the *GPI* Screening[21]

Give the person screened a pen to use so that all responses are recorded without erasures. Record when the person crosses out answers and rewrites them.

This screening should take no longer than ten minutes. When people take longer than ten minutes, you have an indication that the entire *General Processing Inventory (GPI)* should be administered.

Each response should be coded as slow (s) if it takes longer than five seconds. After five slow responses, discontinue the screen. The five slow responses is a positive indicator for the entire *GPI.* You can count 5 seconds silently by saying mentally: *1 Mississippi, 2 Mississippi, 3 Mississippi, 4 Mississippi, 5 Mississippi.*

If a person becomes frustrated taking the screening, discontinue. Ask why the person is frustrated and record the response. The screening should be discontinued when people cannot tolerate it. This is a positive indicator for the entire *GPI.*

Read the words that are in bold and italics. These must be read exactly as written. If the

---

[21] *For questions about scoring and for a complete three-hour GPI evaluation contact* Ruth M. Geiman, Ph.D. at ruthgeiman@yahoo.com.

person screened does not understand what you read, you may then explain the directions and record ED (for "explained directions"). If you need to clarify directions, record your exact clarification. Record any variations from the responses that are typed on the form. Five variations from the answers given are an indicator that the entire *GPI* should be administered.

The answers that are typed are the exact answers that should be given by the person screened. Any variations, however small, should be recorded. They are all errors. For example, these should be recorded on the *GPI* Screening:

- Repeating a number, letter or word (Use R for repeated)
- Asking for the directions again; you are repeating the directions (Use 2x)
- Crossing out answers (X and circle)
- Writing the wrong case of a letter (capital for small or vice versa) (Circle letter and write error)
- Any other variation from the exact letters, numbers, or words required
- Skipping numbers or letters. (X through the letter or number.)
- Slow responses (s)

General Processing Inventory (GPI) **Screening**

Read the directions in italics and bold. You must read these directions **exactly** as written. If you need to explain directions after reading them as written, record that as ED. In addition, record any variations from the answers typed below the directions. Each variation or explanation is an error.

What is your address? (People 10 years and above should include the zip code. Write the exact words.)

Count to thirty. (Record errors. Also, record (s) each time the time between numbers is greater than 5 seconds.)

1 2 3 4 5 6 7 8 9 10 11 12 13 14 15 16 17 18 19 20 21 22 23 24 25 26 27 28 29 30

Count by 2's to twenty (Record errors, but do not count as an error if person begins or does not begin at 0. Record (s) each time the time between numbers is greater than 5 seconds.)

0   2   4   6   8   10   12   14   16   18   20

Count to 100 by 5's. (Record errors. Also, record (s) each time the time between numbers is greater than 5 seconds.)

5 10 15 20 25 30 35 40 45 50 55 60 65 70 75 80 85 90 95 100

Count backwards from 20 to 0. (Record errors. Also, record (s) each time the time between numbers is greater than 5 seconds.)

20 19 18 17 16 15 14 13 12 11 10 9 8 7 6 5 4 3 2 1 0

Count backwards by 2's from 20 to 0. *(Record errors. Also, record (s) each time the time between numbers is greater than 5 seconds.)*

20   18   16   14   12   10   8   6   4   2   0

Count backwards by 5's from 50 to 0. *(Record errors. Also, record (s) each time the time between numbers is greater than 5 seconds.)*

50   45   40   35   30   25   20   15   10   5   0

Spell your name. (Person should spell both first and last names.) *(Record errors. Also, record (s) each time the time between letters is greater than 5 seconds.)*

Give person a sheet of typing paper – unlined. Then say: *Print the capital letters of the alphabet. (Record errors. Also, record (s) each time the time between letters is greater than 5 seconds.)*

A B C D E F G H I J K L M N O P Q R S T U V W X Y Z

Write today's date. (People 10 years old and above should include the year.) *(Record errors. Also, record (s) each time the time between letters and numbers is greater than 5 seconds.)*